Without Apology

By

Charles Davis

Davis Publishing Company

Cover photo by Charles Jordan Davis
Title design by Carter Davis
Cover design by Shenika Harris
Lead Substantive and Copy Editor: Lari-Nicole Kelley
Developmental Editor: Michelle Cerone
Publishing Company: Davis Publishing Company

TABLE OF CONTENTS

PART 3: THE TURNING POINT

Developmental Editor's Note

As an editor, you never know what to expect when you receive a memoir. See, memoirs are bound by the constraints of reality. There are no magical realms. There are no dragons. There are no fairy godmothers. They can feel flat. But this story is more than a memoir. It is a tale of unspeakable trauma and violence, dappled with the pure unshakable joy that is found in the innocence of childhood.

It is a testament to the power of a teacher's love to shape a child's destiny, especially a child born into a world of generational poverty, extreme abuse, relentless bullying, and systemic racism. But above all, it is a bridge—one that says, "I can see your pain. Can you see mine?" It is the missing link between teachers who want to help but don't know how and those children who need their pain seen and understood.

This memoir has the power to reshape a generation, as long as we understand its message—one of intense empathy and compassion the author so freely gives to the people in his life who let him down. There are no fairy godmothers or dragons or magical realms here, but there is plenty of magic.

PROLOGUE

It is my ultimate hope that this memoir will be used as motivation for those who think there is no way out, those who think they have no choice but to live and stay in the truth of their environment. Just because you were raised in a particular area and brought up a certain way does not mean you have to close your mind to the possibility of greatness. You must stay focused on surviving and being a good person, even through the debilitating times of hardship and struggle. You do have what it takes to change your family's legacy.

Not all these stories about my life are good, not all bad, but each is glass shattering in its own way. The idea is to help people across all levels of society take a deep poetic dive into the mind of a young black boy. A look at the overwhelming obstacles that would prove to make me the man I am today. Many of these situations were traumatic and may be difficult to hear. My mind consists of priceless memories of trauma-filled moments.

As a child, these memories stayed hidden behind learning disabilities and behavioral problems from an unforgiving environment that seemed to always be against my journey to greatness. I do not intend to glorify or understate all the major mistakes I made while growing up. The examples told here are some situations that were out of my hands and others I created myself. It is always easy to judge those who come out of similar situations. This book will illuminate how a young boy can be thrust into an environment that will make an animal out of

2

anyone. The decisions you make will determine the type of animal.

Most have no idea the hardships one child can withstand, so hold your judgment until you can see the picture in its entirety. Walking under the cold clouds of that playground filled with traps and temptations makes you aware of the person you must become. That is the person you need to be to survive. When you are forced to tangle with hunger pains and wrestle with the lasting memory of having a gun pointed to your head is when you know.

Many stories of inner-city black youth are negative because of the traumatizing lessons learned in a lifetime. I learned lessons about life, love, trauma, and the importance of mental health. And through these unscrambled words, I have chosen to spell out my story for you.

This book speaks to three critical audiences:

1. The educator believes in educating all who enter the school building. No matter how damaged or difficult they may come.

2. The young person who often feels forgotten and mistreated, who is struggling and begging silently for someone to notice that the problems they are having are real. And they just need an extra push to understand that they can create their own destiny.

3. Any adult in the position to mentor or help guide a young person who they notice struggling.

PART 1
LIFE

CHAPTER 1 | DECISIONS

I am running to the spot where the murder is supposed to occur. Mid-stride, my gun tumbles down my pant leg, hits my shoe, and falls to the concrete. I don't know if it's my nervousness, but it lands without making a sound. I am sweating, and my eyes are watering, but I am unsure why. I bent down to grab the silver .22 I had stolen from my grandfather.

As my hand reached out, it felt like I was moving in slow motion. This is the first person I had ever thought about and planned to kill. I could feel the sun beating down on my neck and the dampness of my clammy hands. My chest was tight, and my mouth was dry. My heart was beating so fast that it felt like it was not beating at all. I continued playing it out in my head as this person got closer. I felt powerful with my arm extended and my hand on the small silver .22 caliber pistol.

Holding it made me feel invincible and unafraid. I was protected but scared at the same time. Here they come; I was just a few steps away from getting this 'muthafucker' that had been messing with me all year. Pulling this trigger will change everything, but I didn't care. Enough was enough. Do I pull it, or do I not? In my head, a voice washed over me, 'Pull that shit nigga. You are here now.'

But how did I even get here? I did not know, did not care, and killing this kid felt like my best option. I'd had enough, but I was about to take someone's ability to reach any life goals. I was going to take away any chance of them growing old and starting a family.

But in my head, I kept thinking, and they should have thought about that before they kept fucking with me. I am sick and tired of this. I told the teachers, and no one did anything about it. What else am I supposed to do? Who can I go to for help? I only told one person about what I was going to do, and he tried to talk me out of it, but I didn't want to listen.

I am about to do what a man must do, especially when I was at the end of my rope and had exhausted all the other options. Time and time again, I found out that no one was going to protect me, not family members, teachers, police, or firefighters. It was time for me to man up and make a name for myself. Time for me to show people that you don't mess with Master Chuck, Sudden Death Jr. Let me rewind and tell you what got me to this point in my life. To the point where I thought the best option was to end another kid's life. Let us start from the beginning.

CHAPTER 2 | RUNNERS READY?

I was born on January 10, 1980, to Charles Sutton and Amanda Davis. The name Charles comes both from my dad and my granddad. My granddad's name is Charles Louis Sutton, Sr., and his nickname was CL. My dad was called Chucky Sutton or 'Sudden Death.'

What kind of a nickname is 'Sudden Death'? I could imagine a girl inviting my dad to her house for the first time and introducing him as 'Sudden Death.' Pretty awkward. The truth of the matter is my dad was a rough character. He was a fighter, and that is how he got his name, 'Sudden Death.' – a tough guy in the neighborhood. Later I would have to pay the price because of his reputation. I got into many fights because people expected me to be as tough as my dad. To tell the difference between me, my younger brother, my dad, and my grandpa, my father's mother decided to call my grandpa 'Chucky Sr.,' my dad 'Big Chuck,' my little brother was "Little Chuck," and I was 'Master Chuck.'

I grew up in Summit Argo, a town located just a stone's throw away from the Chicago line. Summit Argo was also called little Mississippi because of the migration of so many families making a move from Mississippi. My community was built by strong people with challenging backgrounds, but also a community of family and fight. I was built by many hard-working and upstanding families

3

who migrated from Mississippi's harsh realities and racism. Once they arrived in Summit, Illinois, they tried to keep the community family oriented. This area is soaked in the legacies of great people.

This area of Chicago was the stomping grounds and home of Emmett Till and Wheeler Parker. Because of these men, some say that Summit Argo is where great men came from. They were born to change the way the world would look at the city and the movement of life. Emmett Till was only fourteen years old when he was tortured and murdered in Mississippi allegedly for speaking to a white woman while visiting family.

When I learned about Emmett's story at a young age, I always felt a sense of pride while being in that neighborhood and walking the same streets that such a brave young man walked. Elder Wheeler Parker was another great man from Summit Argo. He was born in Schlater, Mississippi, but grew up in Summit Argo, Illinois. Wheeler was Emmett Till's cousin and was with him at the store where the incident took place. Wheeler was more aware of how things were in Mississippi because he had often gone down to spend summers with his uncle. He was able to get away from the situation alive and make it back to Summit, Argo. As Wheeler grew into a responsible young man, he became a prominent leader and Reverend in the community. Anytime you needed anything, you could always go to Reverend Wheeler, and he would always do what he could to help you.

Reverend Wheeler gave me a job at his barbershop when I was about 13, and this step helped contribute to my turning point in life. I made twenty dollars a week to sweep up the hair and keep the pop machine filled. The best benefit was that I could get free haircuts from one of the other barbers named Jarvis. Jarvis always sounded mean but showed me so much, love. He is one of the men in my life that taught me how men are supposed to love. Back then, a black man's love was rough and rugged, the type of love not filled with soft, sensitive words. It was actions, stern discipline, and respect. Jarvis was rooted in sound advice and lessons of right and wrong. Ethics and morals shoved in your face with a side of laughter and get out of my face statements.

I remember walking into the barbershop one rainy day. Jarvis and Rev. Wheeler were cutting hair like always. I walked over to Jarvis and quickly asked if I could get a haircut next. He looked at me as if I had said something wrong. He fired back at me to go do some work and take out the trash. I walked away confused and unsure of why he gave me the response he did because he always gave me haircuts. I came back about thirty minutes later and asked again. He shut off his clippers, slid to the side of his customer, and told me to come here. I walked closer.

"Didn't I tell you to go do some work?" he said. "You come in here splashing water all over the place, and the first thing out of your mouth is can you get a haircut. Who do you think you are?"

I was still confused at why he was chewing me out. I walked away and got back to doing my work. Ten minutes later, after he was done with his customer, he called me back over to his chair. With his old-school raspy voice, "Chucky, come here."

Once I got over there, Jarvis said, "Don't ever come in this shop again without first speaking to Rev. Wheeler, followed by speaking to all the barbers and acknowledging every adult in this shop. Do you understand me? It is called respect, and if you are going to work here, you are going to have some."

And before I could get a word out, he said, "Now go take out the rest of that garbage."

I had a stunned look on my face because I did not realize that I had done something wrong. I dropped my head and began to walk away, but as I was doing that, Jarvis then added, "and when you get done with the garbage, get over here so I can give you a haircut."

So I did just that–finished with the trash and then immediately got in Jarvis's chair for my cut. Once the haircut started, the lesson started. Now he would talk with a lower tone, more compassionate and kinder. Told me how important it was for me as a young man to always understand how to enter a room with adults in it. He asked if I understood what he was saying and why. I shook my head to say yes, I understood.

And out of nowhere, he popped the back of my neck and said, "Does your mouth work? Then use it to say yes, sir."

I laughed and said, "Yes, sir," as I sat back and continued my cut. It was lessons like this that I would experience throughout my life that would shape me into the man I would become. The question is would I become this man in time to save my life?

My mom had my siblings and me when she was very young—the first being Tasha. My mom was fifteen years old when my sister was born. Tasha is about as tough as any woman that I have ever known. I watched my big sister beat everybody up. I mean, she could fight like no other. I have watched her beat up girls, boys, grown men, and anybody else who wanted to test her. My sister Tasha used to fight all my battles when she was around. Tasha was an intelligent kid but high-tempered, easy to provoke, and very hard to calm down. My mom was sixteen years old when she gave birth to me. After I was born, my mother had four more boys. Taiwan, Wayne, Joe, and Keon. I will tell you guys about them later. Because of having children at such a young age, my mom and dad never graduated from high school. We did not have much money, and this set the stage for some strenuous times.

I remember the colorless, blandly decorated government products that filled our cabinets and bellies. As much as we hated it, that government cheese made the best-grilled cheese sandwiches and baked macaroni. When we would get hungry, we would sneak into the kitchen and pinch off the corners of the block of cheese. Every month we would get whooped for that; you would think we would learn sooner or later. But no, we did it again and again. It was like a ritual when the beginning of the month came. The cheese arrived, and we would start sneaking into the kitchen one by one, taking our turn pinching off chunks of this massive block of cheese. Our mother would open the refrigerator and notice the patches of cheese missing. Then she would call us over and ask who was pinching off the cheese, but like every other month, we looked around like we didn't know what she was talking about, and so the butt whippings would start. I laugh at this today because you would think we would have learned our lesson.

I wonder what we hated more: the cheese or the bulky box of powdered milk; it did not matter how much water you added to it, it was still the worst substitution for real milk. I would often revert to using water in my cereal. Another staple we loved was syrup sandwiches. We would eat so many syrup sandwiches; the whole loaf of bread would be gone before we knew it. Then when my mom came into the kitchen to make a sandwich for herself or add a few pieces of bread to my dad's dinner, she would notice that it was long gone. I remember going into stores and supplementing the welfare products that we received from the government by stealing food to survive. The choice was often ours when it came to what it was that we wanted to eat as long as we made the trip to the store to steal it.

I had gotten so good at stealing I would go into the store and walk around for a few minutes, checking out who was there. Looked out for certain people that would watch us closer, and there were others who had no clue what we were there to do. One morning I got up with hunger on my mind. As I entered the store, I still did not have a clear idea of what I wanted to eat, but my legs moved me to the sandwich meat section. So that is what I got, a few packs of sandwich meat, and then I moved to the section with the sweets.

I quickly hid a few honey buns in my pants and then started to move towards the door. As I was walking out, someone called my name, and I knew I was about to get busted. But it was someone from the store asking me to tell my mom hi. That was an easy request as I continued to leave the store. Cutting it close like always, never knowing the day I would actually get caught. There were a lot of us to feed, and it was not often that we had snacks or good food in the house to eat. Whenever we did, it would be gone as quickly as it appeared. We were young savages, and we were determined to get what we wanted, even if it was just a cookie or two. Every time I was in the house, I was reminded of the grim reality of our situation. I quickly understood that we did not have as much as other kids had at a young age. The empty cabinets and barren refrigerator dared us to dream of something more.

But outside was a different story. Outside took away my sense of being poor; I felt like I was on an equal playing field. Outside of the house, I could be free of the bonds of poverty with all the sadness, oppression, and the negative limitation of permanent lack. Still, outside provided the promise of freedom—the freedom to dream, make-believe, and be a kid having fun. I could smile outside the door of the oppressive reality, hunger, and pain.

Those were the fun days; despite not having much, we found ways to stay entertained. We lived in a neighborhood where everyone knew everyone. We met up with friends searching for the same escape we sought outside, and they were like an extended family.

The outsiders did not know the horrors of our inside world. On the outside, our embarrassment was our own making, not caused by our parents. Our parents were so scarred by their beginnings and failings they had no concept of how the cycle of poverty had hypnotized them into this way of life. Cruel reality released me, and I could let my imagination soar to magical places of happiness. I could be whoever I wanted to be. We had immense fun and laughter that brought me the type of joy that helped me to get through any hardship that my oppression and depression could ever dish out.

While outside, poverty was a distant place that no longer had a hold on me. I would make gun-shaped slingshots that we would use to shoot the caps off pop cans at each other. We ran all day and played football or basketball. We would find old mattresses that people would throw away, and we would spend hours flipping on the smelly pee stained cushions. These were the things to do back then, and we could not wait to get outside to do them.

We ran all day and played football or basketball. We would go in and out of friends' houses, playing video games or eating their food. Some friends even had cable, which meant we could watch rap videos.

I know most people want you to believe that the narrative of the inner-city is one of destruction, violence, and drugs, but this is not that story, not exactly. There are so many shades of grey in that black and white narrative some people want you to believe. However, those excuses are not entirely true.

My mom and my step-grandmother were in labor at the same time, so I was actually older than one of my uncles. Lil Charlie's wife, Willamae, gave birth to my uncle shortly after I was born. Granted, it was only by a few minutes, but I never let him forget that. We would grow up together and would go outside and wrestle, pretending to be Hulk Hogan and Ultimate Warrior. We loved WWF, which is now called WWE. The imaginary life was outside, and I couldn't wait to get to it. We would literally play all day long back then. I smile, thinking about it still. But we knew at the end of the night, we would have to enter the environment of those unforgiving walls of poverty and abuse.

I have heard people say, 'you never know what is going on in someone's house – behind closed doors. In our house, it was the lack of food, trauma, pain, and constant bad news. I remember how upset we all were when we found out that we were moving to Milwaukee, Wisconsin. During this move, we made that ride stuck in the back of a crowded dark U-Haul. Once we arrived at the new apartment, we would find out that we would spend almost all of the 24 hours of every day stuck in the back room– a room filled with two twin mattresses placed on the floor with three or four sheets for my siblings and me. There was a TV sitting on a crate with aluminum foil wrapped around the antennas. This was our life, with no toys and not much outside time.

We could never understand why we were not allowed to go outside much. We would look out the window and watch other kids play in the snow. My brothers would ask some of the kids to throw snowballs up to our window, and we would catch them and play with the snow inside our room. The joy of just having a piece of the outside was all we needed to get through the day. Even on the days that were supposed to be amazing, there would always be something to come and snatch the joy away.

My birthday had come around, and to my surprise, my mom had bought me a cake. As we were in the living room singing happy birthday, my mom's boyfriend called her a few times, and she did not answer right away. That made him upset because she was taking too long, so he came into the living room and punched her in the face, flipping the table over that had my beautiful cake on it. Grabbed my mom and dragged her off into the bedroom, where he would continue to hit her repeatedly. I was fearful but had grown tired of it; I walked over to the door and began yelling and banging on the door. Her boyfriend came to the door and slapped me as hard as he could. That was all it took for me to hit the floor. Once there, he gave me one swift kick to the stomach and then disappeared back to the room. I laid there and cried like a punk, not being able to protect myself or my mother. The move did not last longer than a year because of the turmoil that continued to brew within our home between my mother and her abusive boyfriend. So, we were off, moving back to Illinois.

I was the typical young black boy born and raised in and around Chicago. Far too often, kids like me did not have a chance at fulfilling our dreams, by no fault of our own. That was the life we expected, and most learned to live with it. We never went on family vacations since we could barely keep food on the table most weeks. Growing up, my parents never helped me with my schoolwork and hardly ever spoke positive words to me. I had adapted to that life and learned to make the best of what I had without expectations from the adults in my life. I would wake up each morning and hope for a good day, but not often would that wish come true.

I did live in a community that cared about its children, but often many of us would fall through the cracks of inner-city struggles. My mother was a daughter of a self-proclaimed pimp named Little Charlie. My grandparents wanted to be there for me, but they were trying to make things happen for themselves; they did not have the resources to provide for me.

Top left to right: brothers and I, Wayne, Me, and Taiwan.
Bottom left to right: brother Joe, nephew Hollis, and brother Keon

CHAPTER 3 | DEAR MAMA

There will be quite a few stories throughout this book that may depict my mother in a negative light. Although this was the case in many situations when I was young, it is not a direct reflection of the woman she is today. She is a loving grandmother and an amazing mother.

My parents were products of their environment in a culture where mothers and fathers were still kids themselves, without the guidance of parenting experience. My grandmother Lil Freddie was a young lady who fell head over heels in love with Little Charlie while in her mid-teens. And my mother would soon repeat the same mistake. Just like my grandmother, she too would quickly become a child raising babies.

My mother, Amanda Denise Davis, known as "Neese" in the neighborhood, was born to my granny and grandpa Freddy Mae Davis and Charlie Harris on November 29, 1962. My mother started life on a rough foot, just like most in the neighborhood during that time.

Her own mother was a beautiful young butterfly. But she was unmarried and dealing with my grandfather, Lil Charlie, who was not a good man or father, mainly because of his sneaking around and being with other women. Lil Charlie was a man of many talents and often maintained relationships with multiple women. He was a clean-dressed, smooth-talking, tough ladies' man.

To understand my mother's life, we have to understand the shoes she had to walk in. My mother, the first girl, was expected to be the most responsible, often home babysitting her younger sister and brother. When my granny would get home, she would give her two dollars and tell her to get something to eat for everyone, and before she could get back, her mom was dressed and gone.

My mom loved to sneak out of the house. Her younger brother called her a nighthawk who hated to get home on time. My mom would tell me stories of how my granny would have to come to her hangout spots and force her to come home. She wanted to experience having a childhood of her own without the pressures of being responsible for her younger siblings.

My mom loved to be social with friends or whoever she was dating at the time. They would spend too much time hanging out in places they probably should not have been. My mom often spoke about hanging out by the car wash or at the bar at a young age. My grandmother Lil Freddie said there was nothing but trouble in both places. There was drinking, smoking, and sex, and my grandmother didn't want my mom to fall into any of these habits. To this day, my mom speaks highly of one of her best friends, Cynthia "Pooty" Armstrong, whom she spent a lot of time with. We could only wonder what would happen at some of these parties.

But when I would ask my mom, all she would say was that they were all out there being fast and doing shit they should not have been doing. My mom claimed to have a bad memory when I found out more about her young wild days—even telling me to shut up and leave her alone a few times. We both laughed out loud and continued talking about those days.

Soon, my mom was stuck on a boy in the neighborhood known for being a tough guy that no one wanted to mess with—Chucky Sutton, my father. Chucky had a few girlfriends he was dating at the time, but his constant fights with them left room for my mom to swoop down like a hawk and take her place as his new main woman.

My mom did well in school up until she reached high school. She was smart and liked school, even wanting to be a future nurse, but since her mom did not push for college, she did not consider it an option. She also experienced her first setback: getting pregnant very young with my sister.

At 15 years old, my mom went into her mother's room to ask why she had not had a period for a few months. She says her mom responded that she did not know and did not have time to talk about something so dumb. My mother thought maybe it was something normal, so she wasn't too worried about it. My grandma wondered why my mom could not keep up with her own time of the month.

She did not find out she was pregnant until she was about three and a half months. My mom says she remembers she was surprised but not scared. She was just a little nervous because she did not know what to expect at an early age. She was young and thin, and no one could tell she was with child at the time.

Once her mother found out, she told her she would be the one to take care of the baby, so do not ask her to watch any babies! Because of this early blessing, my mom felt the need to drop out of high school. At 15, before her sophomore year, my mom called it quits. She had no one who could babysit for her, and no one tried to talk her out of dropping out. Unfortunately, my mom did not have extensive knowledge of how to raise us kids to survive the cruelty of America. It's just the way things were during those times. Kids were raising kids—babies raising babies. Even speaking to my grandma, she would tell me how tough it was to have children at a young age. She has admitted to not knowing a lot about bringing up kids at that time, either. It was a generational thing; she tried the best that she could. As she grew older and started helping to raise her grandchildren, her true abilities how in raising a young black child began to shine.

Thrust into full-time motherhood, there would be a tight clap on the sneaking out late at night. But this would not stop my mom; she would continue stealing her mother's clothes and throwing them out of the window so they would be waiting for her outside. Once the coast was clear, my mom was out the window. And with a quick change of clothes, the young nighthawk had transformed into the woman she had imagined. Free and beautiful, wanted by all the young men. From the words of my uncle Edward, she was always dressing fly and was very tough. He says they all get their ability to dress slick from my grandad.

She had her share of fist fights in the middle of the ashy concrete, surrounded by the sparkle of the streetlights that lit up the makeshift ring of glory in the hood. My mom and I spoke of a time when she got into a fight with my father's other girlfriend because she was disrespectful. My mom would not back down from any challenge, and just like the rest of us, she had to grow and learn life's lessons.

Compounding that she had us at such a young age, she also had quite a few barriers to work through. My mom did not have the skills or support to hold a meaningful job during these early years, which mainly made her dependent on other men like my father for help. While meticulously guiding herself through all the traps that are often set up for a young black woman, my mother pushed herself to be the best mom she knew how.

She spoke about the lack of education and lessons that her mom taught her. She said she had to learn everything through trial and error. While fighting the urges that most teenagers battled against, she both chased and ran from negative things in her life. Sometimes she caught what she was seeking, and other times, she was caught up by what she was running to escape, which was often the love and affection from a man who had no idea how to treat her.

I have never resented my mother for the mistakes she made. As I am writing about my childhood trauma, she, too, had to deal with the shattering effects of a set of parents that were not the greatest when it came to an understanding of how to raise children at such a young age. In her story alone, we can find the magnificent strength of a woman with almost no shot.

Having learned what my mom went through and seeing it with my own eyes, I know that she was looking for an escape from her trauma. I watched and heard my mom get beaten by men more times than I could count. I have even brought some of these moments up to her, and she did not remember some of them. It made me so sad that she had forgotten. Had it happened so much that a beating was relegated to a forgettable memory? Had she been desensitized to being punched in the face? Had she manufactured a culture of painless nerves and thoughts?

I can remember after being beaten by my father one night in the motel, she woke up the following morning and made him breakfast, and just like that, she had moved on with her day and life. Had it not been a concern of hers anymore?

I remember times when all my mom wanted to do, was laugh aloud. She is silly in that way, usually always happy. When she was younger, she tended to do what she had to do for her boyfriend at the time. She was a follower, a follower of love. I saw my mother give up so much of herself so that she could please a bunch of no-good men. I saw my mother attempt to do the right things multiple times, only to have one of those men tell her to do it differently.

Based on what I know, what I saw, and what mistakes I have made as a child and an adult, I can never blame my mother for the mistakes she made when she was young.

Mother, never let people weaponize your past against your future. You are an amazing and strong woman, and I love you for the lessons you taught me as a kid and the ones you still teach me today. You are one of the loveliest women I know, and I am so proud of you for your growth and accomplishments. I see you, and I know you will only get better.

Pictures of my mother, Amanda "Neese" Davis

CHAPTER 4 | SUDDEN DEATH

I sat in the car watching and listening while my father was standing on the porch talking to another man through the screen door. I heard him say, "Come outside for a minute so we can talk." The man would not come outside, and they continued to argue on each side of the door, making sure to hold their own space.

The scene was set. Raindrops appeared to fall in slow motion to create an ominous haze. I looked down to see my dad's boot untied with the tongue folded down just enough that it captured the end of his pant leg. He was a good-sized man, so his pants fit snugly. Built like a tree that would not move if a car rammed it. His old and stained wife-beater screamed for the washing machine, but his massive arms would not allow for regular white tee shirts.

The yelling continued as I heard him say, "I need my fucking money." And then, out of nowhere, his arm reached back and extended forward as he punched the man right in the face through the screen door. The motion ripped the net off the screen door, shattered the glass, and bent the frame away from the bolts. The man fell to the floor while my dad casually walked back to the car as if nothing had just happened. I asked him how much money the man owed him, and he said, "It doesn't matter how much money they owe you. It matters that they pay it back like they said they would."

I experienced a lot of different situations that I would have loved to have my father to guide me through like I had seen so many times from the great fathers on TV. But unfortunately, situations like these are all I have left. Aggression, abuse, and absence are my most distinctive memories. I had to tackle all the negative lessons and examples I was shown as a kid with very little consistent positive guidance. I was left wondering which examples about life to copy and which to replace with a better decision.

Unfortunately, I did not get a chance to speak to my father much about why he may have thought he had the personality and character he had. My father himself was a troubled man. He was aggressive and experienced a lot of pain throughout his young life. He was the smallest of his three brothers but would get beat just as severely as they did.

My father grew up with working parents who provided everything they needed. There were meals on the table and clothes on their backs. He and his brothers had positive role models in their lives, but their father was the problem in the household. He could not shake his demons which made him act out on the family.

My grandad C.L. would often come home in a bad mood. He would then transfer that anger and frustration to his wife and sons. My grandad did not like anyone to talk back to him or allow them to speak their mind. He was old-school and believed that the man ran the household and everyone in it.

One day, my grandad came home from being out most of the day. My Grandma Helen was cooking dinner as the boys were preparing the table. Once the table was ready, everyone sat down to eat. My grandad, father, and two uncles were sitting at the table. Once dinner was ready, she set the pot of food in the middle of the table so that everyone could serve themselves. She took a seat at the other end of the table as the boys started to fill their plates.

Grandad asks, "What are we having?"

Grandma Helen replied, "Chili."

He was not in the mood for chili, so he asked, "Why the hell are we eating chili?"

She replied, "We are eating chili, and if you don't want it, then don't eat it." My grandma, being the tough woman that I remember her being, must have been getting tired of my grandfather because this was not her usual response to her husband.

"What did you say to me?" my grandfather C.L. responded.

"We are eating chili, and if you don't want it, then don't eat it," she repeated. That was the wrong thing to say to him.

"Who the hell are you talking to?" he yelled as he got up and walked to the other end of the table. My father and uncles all looked at each other with worried eyes. They knew what talking back to him meant for whoever was bold enough to do it.

Once he reached my grandma, he planted his leg firmly, and with a quick and powerful thrust, he extended his arms with the speed of lightning. His hands connect to my grandma's chest and shoulder, pushing her and the chair she was sitting on to the floor. She hit the floor hard as the chair stumbled to her side. He yelled at her and continued to move toward her. He bent over and clenched his hands around her neck. He began to choke her, which made my father and uncles furious!

My father jumped up and attempted to help his mom. Running towards his dad, but with a quick thrust of his fist, my father's body received the blow that stopped him in his tracks. My uncle said incidents like this caused my dad to make the mental adjustments necessary to protect himself. My dad could not help his mom very much, but it was only because of his size, not his heart. My dad took a lot of beatings as a kid, but he always took them as a man and did not complain. But this did cause an everlasting trauma in my father. It hardened him and made him cold.

As the years passed, he finally had a growth spurt around the age of 15, and then he was just as big as his father. He was no longer the little kid that could not protect himself or his mother. He was big, strong, and had experienced enough abuse to take a stand. It was his turn to defend himself and his mother.

My dad embodied his massive reputation for being tough. No one wanted to mess with him, and if you were a friend of his, you would never have to worry about anyone bothering you. It was said that even if you were not his close friend if someone was bullying you, you could tell Big Chuck, and he would come and kick their ass for you. He got his nickname, Sudden Death, because of the speed and sheer ferocity he used to demolish his opponent in a fight.

These are not stories told by him with embellishments; they are from some of the actual people he had beaten up. In my opinion, you know you were a legend when guys were proud to have been beaten up by you.

When I got to school, teachers would always ask me who my dad was; when I told them, they would instantly judge me. Automatically they assumed I would be a tough kid who caused trouble. Most of the time, this assumption was valid, but it was not because I wanted to be that way.

With the trauma my dad had experienced as an abused child, I genuinely think he transformed from sweet and caring to angry and brutal. He didn't understand how to break that cycle; he was conditioned to believe that you had to be more aggressive than the rest to survive. I don't know if I had ever seen my dad cry, get scared, or show a soft side. I don't recall a single time when he told me he loved me or my brothers and sisters.

I believe his brutal childhood did not allow him to bounce back into being a success in a society that did not give black men an equal chance. My dad had been through a lot in a short period of his life. He left high school and went to the military, searching for clarity and a career. This did not last long, so he was back right away.

My dad worked odd jobs to make money, mainly as a bouncer in the club scene and construction jobs here and there. I remember my dad took my siblings and me to the beach down on the lakefront in Chicago one hot summer. We had so much fun. Believe it or not, that is the only fun memory I can recall having with my father. There could have been more, but I cannot remember any other positive memory.

My father was not present much at all. After the early years, he just wasn't around much, some due to us moving out of Summit Argo to Joliet, Illinois, and other times because he would be somewhere else.

Everything I can remember of my dad, he was a harsh jerk, but we understood that he loved us in his own way. As so many children do, we find a reason to see good in our absent or abusive fathers. Maybe we gave him credit because we could see the stress of life that is sometimes applied tenfold to a black man, especially in those times. Perhaps it was just that we begged for any form of love from our father. It is safe to say I had a love-hate relationship with my father. I loved him because he was my father, and at the same time, I hated his guts because of the pain he caused my mom.

My dad beat my mom brutally and was relentless when the fights started. The first clear memory of this is when he sent a hard blow to her stomach immediately followed by a punch to the side of the face, and down she went. I watched with my hands covering my face, and a sharp pain rushed through my head and heart.

Even as a small child, I felt that intense need to protect my mother. "Stop hitting my momma," I yelled.

His eyes quickly tracked the sound, and he found me standing by the bathroom. A sheet was lying on the floor where my brothers and sister had been asleep. His massive body headed my way, and I remember his shadow covering me before reaching me. Then he slapped the soul out of my body, and I hit the floor hard. He moved back to continue his assault on my mother's body as I lay there.

I do not even remember my age, but I remember praying for my mother to leave him or kill him. There was a rage inside of me that I could not explain. I had never felt this feeling before. It was new but addictive, and I wanted to feel it again, even though the feeling scared me.

After each beating, I could not understand how she could lay in the same bed as him. Then they would wake up in the morning as if nothing had ever happened, and the only evidence that remained of the terrifying fight was her bruised ribs and a black eye that was swollen shut.

My father did not purposely teach me many lessons, but the ones he did teach me were memorable. I could understand at that moment how my father felt when he was a child and could not defend his mother while my grandfather was beating her. But I could never understand how he could turn around and cause the same pain to another woman after witnessing his own mother go through it.

Choosing not to become the type of man I experienced with my father is the greatest lesson he taught me. Most prominently, I vowed never to make a woman in my life feel the terror and show the fear my mother did so often. She was afraid for her life regularly. She moved in fear and spoke with fear every time he was near. Her life paused when he was around, and she walked on eggshells, but still, it was not enough to protect her. Everything was about him, and I hated him for this. I used to tell myself regularly that I would have to kill this man one day.

Having this thought about my father was heavy, but after watching this man repeatedly and savagely beat my mother, it was the only way I thought I could stop him. His time would come, and I just hoped to be a part of the destruction. How is a young boy supposed to function with these intrusive thoughts? I loved my father, but I hated his actions. I felt displaced when he could come around. I wanted to love him. I wanted a hug from my dad, just to see what it felt like, and maybe it would calm the demons he was facing. But within minutes of him being around, I wanted to punch him and cause him the same pain he so often caused our family.

When growing up with abusive parents, there are two paths for one to take. My father chose the path of becoming the abuser to dominate his women and children with the same abuse he experienced as a child. Then there is the path of peace. To make the active choice to use your bad experiences for good, to become the best version of yourself for your family. You can choose to make sure your family never experiences the terror of abuse that you once felt.

I cannot understand what can make a person who has felt the pain and fear of abuse be able to grow up and cause that same pain and fear in their own family. Choose to be better. You do not have to follow the cycle of abuse. Learn your triggers and how to communicate appropriately. Make sure you keep your anger in check with your spouse and children so that they never feel or see that fear you once experienced.

Note to self... always be a better man than my father.

Uncle Keith, my dad, Uncle Darrell

Chucky "Sudden Death" Sutton

Grandmother Helen and Grandfather

Charles "Sudden Death" Sutton

CHAPTER 5 | 1ST MEMORY OF PAIN

My first memory of pain happened at an early age. I was born into a situation that moved like a Nascar race, with three siblings born within five years. There was a move out of my grandmother Lil Freddie's house that would take us to a home by the railroad tracks.

I was very hungry at the time and could not find anything to eat, so I took it upon myself to go to the store up the street on the corner. Once inside, I started taking candy off the shelf and putting it in my pocket. How else would I silence this scream for food in my belly? Unfortunately, I was caught stealing the items, and the store clerk walked me home and told my mom.

The clerk left, and my mom went to her room to get a belt and came back and started beating me. I couldn't take it anymore, so I got up and started to run. She got angrier because she couldn't catch me.

Whether on purpose or because she dropped it, she took the belt and turned it upside down, so the buckle was now on the end of contact. She held on tight and started swinging as I attempted to dodge and duck out of the way. But with her repeated swings, the belt buckle connected to my upper face. I quickly dropped to the floor and grabbed my face. My mom came to stand over me and delivered several more strikes to my whole body with the buckle. To this day, I bear the scar on my face from that buckle.

That is the earliest memory of my first beating, but there were so many more to come. I tend to make many excuses for my mom for why we got our whippings. Maybe it's a son's love type of thing, not wanting to make his mom out to be a bad person. There were many times that I felt that because there were so many boys in my family, my mom felt like she had to punish us the way she did. I felt like my mom had to go to the extreme to show us that we would not get away with anything.

Sometimes my mom would take my brothers and me to sit in the bathtub, get out one at a time, and then she would whip us each as we got out. We would sit in the bathtub arguing over who would go first or last, depending on the mood we thought she was in. Depending on if we thought the beatings would last a long time or be over quick. It was different each time, and sometimes we would guess wrong.

We also experienced getting beaten while my mom would sit on our heads and shoulders. This happened because we would often take off running, and my mom did not want to chase after us. She would make us lay across the bed while she physically sat on our heads and shoulders while hitting us.

As I said, some things done to us were caused by our actions. But could we have gone without the beatings? Would speaking to and trying to understand us have helped more than being physically punished? There is not a single time I can tell you that I remember my mom or dad telling my siblings or me that they loved us. I am sure they did, but it is crazy that I do not have a memory of that. Maybe that is what we were missing. What came first, the chicken or the egg? Meaning, did we, the children, do things because of how we were treated and because of the way we did not feel loved? Or did we get treated the way we did because we were rough as hell? An interesting question to dive into, which we will hopefully, by the end of this book, get a grip on which it may be.

As memorable as this experience was, what stands out to me is the next time I went to school after this event. A teacher noticed my face, and the look she gave me was filled with genuine sadness. It was the first time I remember seeing a teacher look at me like they cared about me.

This memory stands out because the teacher never said anything about the marks on my face and body, but she walked over to me, hugged me, and said she had brought me something. She showed me that she cared, even if she didn't address it directly. It made me feel special and took my mind off my face and the beating I had gotten the day before. All she did was give me some candy and a hug. She always had my favorite, which was Now-and-Later's.

It changed my mood and the course of the day. It changed the way I felt about myself and how I felt about her. I don't think I had any bad feelings for her, but honestly, I do not believe she was ever really on my radar as one of my favorite teachers. But this simple action had changed everything.

This simple action was the first time I had experienced the power of a positive teacher and the impact they could have on me. I am sure I started to get on that teacher's nerves because I came to her for every problem. But I had finally found someone I could talk to, someone I trusted and could ask for help.

Teachers, sometimes you may see something you know is out of place, but directly asking may not be the best approach in some situations. Show love, kindness, and acknowledgment but don't start by prying. Let that child know they are cared for and build their trust. With that trust will soon come communication.

CHAPTER 6 | UNWANTED TOUCHES

When I was seven, something changed for us; we were no longer living in the house by the railroad tracks. Although the house was a tiny two-room flat, we were used to it, and it was home. It is the first place I could remember living. I remember the brown, well-cushioned couch that would sink in when we played a doctor on it and the round table, I would run around to get away from my mom's whoopins. The small refrigerator that would hold the block of government cheese in it was tall enough to stack the powdered milk on top and out of reach of us kids.

After we moved, I could no longer hear the sounds of steel against steel, as the train rails would vibrate myself and our roaches to sleep. The comfort of a morning train passing by and the smell of the exhaust from diesel trucks as they would rev up for their morning runs was gone.

For some reason, we had moved to a nearby motel where we would live for several weeks. The motel was in Summit Argo but a little further from the neighborhood with our family and friends. Sometimes my dad would pop up and stay the night with my mom, but most of the time, it would just be my mom and us. That was a time when the food supply was very short for my siblings and me. We were often left alone at this hotel without much food and would love to go to school simply because we knew we would get to eat lunch. We ate as much as we could at school because we knew once back at the motel that there would not be much food to eat, if any.

I was too young to understand the shift in the lack of food. But later, speaking to my mother about this situation, she explained that she did not do what she was supposed to do to stay in the government program that allowed us to receive free food. The milk and cheese products had come in handy while we were younger, and being at this motel without it would stress the importance of it. However, my food problem was about to change for the better, but I did not know what it would cost me.

One day after school, I made peanut butter, jelly, and banana sandwich with the supplies I found in our room. I took my plate and sat on the bed to watch one of my favorite cartoons, which at the time was Thundercats. As I prepared to take my first bite, I looked down at the bread to see a big piece of mold. I thought it was only on some of the bread, so I pinched that part off and ate the rest of it without looking.

At that point, I was not in the business of wasting any food since we didn't know when we would get more. Within a few minutes, the whole sandwich was gone, and I was enjoying my cartoons. I am unsure if it was the mold or something else was wrong with my stomach, but it started hurting badly. I tried to go to the bathroom, which didn't help, so I went outside to try and play the pain off by running around. Nothing helped the stomach pains, and I headed back to the room, leaning against the wall as I was walking, holding my stomach. One of the ladies who worked at the motel saw me and called me over. I am not sure if this lady was a receptionist or a maid. I just knew that she lived in the motel also.

"What is wrong?" she asked.

I replied, "My stomach hurts. I just finished eating a peanut butter, jelly, and banana sandwich, and there was a little mold on the bread."

"Well, all of that stuff may be why your stomach is hurting," she said. "Would you like something to make it feel better?"

"Yes," I answered.

"Come with me," she directed as we began to walk to her room, where she went in for a couple minutes. She came back and gave me some water that looked frizzy and bubbly. It was making a weird sound.

"What is this?" I asked as I inspected the contents of the glass.

"Alka-Seltzer," she replied, "just drink it, and it will make you feel better."

I drank a little bit, and it was nasty. It bubbled in my mouth, fizzy and sour, but I drank it anyway. Honestly, I don't remember if it worked or not, but I drank it. A day or two later, I saw the lady again.

"How are you feeling today?" she asked when she saw me.

"I feel good today," I replied.

"Have you had anything to eat today?" she asked.

As I looked down at my shoes, "No, not yet."

"What is your favorite food?" she asked as she looked down at me.

"Cereal or peanut butter and jelly sandwiches," I replied with a smile.

She asked, "Would you like a peanut butter and jelly sandwich now?"

"Yes, please!" I responded, with much excitement.

She smiled and said, "Come on," and we walked back over to her room, where she asked me to come in. We went inside, and as she began making a sandwich. The lights were very dim, and there was one bed. There was a lot of food on the counter, and the TV was loud. The room had a weird smell to it. I could not tell what the smell was from, but I couldn't stand the smell. She gave me the sandwich, and as I walked out of the door, she asked me, "Aren't you gonna give me a hug before you leave?"

I answered, "Sure." I hugged her and left.

I did not know that would be the start of something very dark. It would be an early beginning of a situation that never should happen to any child. A situation that far too many kids are forced to go through, one that leaves a lasting impact on their entire lives. This is an experience that I can trace as the root of many issues I have had as an adult.

For the next few days, I was experiencing this feeding feast, but some form of touch always followed. Because we did not have much food, I would continue to go to this lady's room. I wanted to stop going, but I felt trapped because now she wasn't just giving me enough food for myself, she was giving me food to go for my brothers and sister, so I continued to go. The food she was giving me was beginning to add up, and my siblings were getting excited. We had sandwiches, candy, cookies, juice boxes, and all the luxurious stuff for a kid. Every time I would go to her room, she would give me something but always asked for a hug in return.

I would hug her around the waist, and other times she would kneel over on her knees, and I would hug her neck. Soon the hugs grew longer. Sometimes she would take my head and put it against her chest.

Several days had gone by. She would feed me often, and I would give her hugs each time. She gave me a snack this particular time, but she asked if I would stay in her room and eat. I hated being in the room, but I knew I had to endure to get food for my siblings and me. I sat on the floor and ate as she played my favorite cartoons on the TV.

I finished eating, and I got up to get ready to leave, she asked if I had gotten full, and I replied, "Yes." As I was leaving, she reminded me about her hug.

As I got to her, she said, "We're going to try something a little different this time since I gave you more food than I normally give you."

"Okay," I responded, and I hugged her.

She looked at me in my face and said, "Give me a kiss on the cheek."

I did as she asked, and then she asked if she could give me one. I said yes because I did not know what else to say. After the kiss on the cheek, she grabbed my ears to look at me right in my face and gave me a soft kiss on the lips. I thought it was odd, and I did not like it. This had been my first kiss, and it was from a grown-up. I took the food she had given me for my siblings and left the room. They were so excited because of all the food I was bringing back. But I was wondering if I should tell someone about the kiss. The next day I was outside playing, and she called me over.

I walked with her to her room, and she said, "Have a seat. I will make you something to eat." She began making me a sandwich as I was watching TV. She brought me the sandwich, but I noticed she did not have her shirt on this time. She was only wearing a bra as she sat watching over me like a lioness watching over one of her cubs. I could feel her looking at me, watching me eat. After a minute had passed, she came over and started to rub my head. I ate the sandwich as I was watching TV. I got up to leave, and again she asked me for a hug. She squatted down on her knees so that I could hug her. I wasn't sure how to hug her while not wearing a shirt. I did not want to touch where I was not supposed to accidentally. I remember reaching up to her neck to avoid her chest.

"No, it's okay, you can hug me like this," as she put my arms under her arms so I would wrap them around her back. It put my face close to her breasts. I was lost and unsure what to think about what was going on. I just remember they were huge. I guess at that age, they all looked big.

She asked, "How do you feel?"

"Fine," I responded because I thought I had to.

She said, "Okay, give me a kiss." I kissed her on the lips, and then I left, not thinking anything of it. When the following day came, she saw me and said, "Don't forget to come by for your snack later." I went to get my snack, but things were different. Usually, she would start making the sandwich and preparing the snacks. However, this time she told me to sit on the bed, and she came over and sat next to me. She started to rub the top of my head. I didn't know what to think of it. I just sat there and watched TV as if nothing was happening.

As she got up and started to make food for me, she asked, "Is there anything special I would like to eat?"

"Yes," I replied. "I would like a peanut butter and jelly sandwich with cookies and juice."

She said, "Okay, I will make it for you. Just give me one second."

She left the room and went into the bathroom. When she came back, she had on a robe. She walked over to me as she was holding onto the robe and said, "What did you say you wanted to eat again?" I repeated what I had asked for. She said, "Well, I need you to do something for me first before I make your sandwich." She had caught me on a rough day, and I think she knew it. I was starving and was desperate to get this food.

"What do you want me to do?" I asked.

She responded, "I hurt my back and need you to rub it."

I said, "Okay, I will."

She then opened her housecoat and slid it down to her waist, but she didn't have anything under it. At that point, I didn't know what to do. I just stood there frozen in my place. "Don't be scared," she said. "Have you ever seen a lady with no shirt on before?"

"No," I responded, trying to look anywhere but at her.

"It's not a big deal; all boys have to see ladies without a shirt on sooner or later," she said. "Let's just make it easier. You can take off your shirt too." I did as she told me to. As she moved toward me, she asked, "Have you ever touched a lady's breast before?"

At that point, I did not know what to say. I just stood there and stared at her in shock. I was at a loss for words. I mumbled, "No," while shaking my head. I was looking around for a way to escape.

As she reached for me, she said, "Give me your hand." Then she took hold of my hand and placed it on her breast. I moved my hand immediately.

"You don't have to be scared," she said. "You are a big boy, and you have to act like one. You are not a baby anymore." The force of the words that came out of her mouth next made me act accordingly. "Give me your hand, but do not move it so fast this time." She put it back onto her breast, and I left it there for what felt like 10 minutes. I was no longer nervous. At this point, I was more scared and confused that I had just done something wrong. She said with praise, "Don't be scared. You did a good job. I feel better now. Come give me a kiss and a hug, and I'll make your sandwich." So once again, I did as she requested. My chest was pressed against her chest, both of us without shirts on. She asked again, "Do you still want your sandwich?"

I nodded, "Yes." She then placed both of my hands on her breast and had me massage them. I removed my hands, and I just stood there.

She said, "Thank you. You did a good job. That wasn't so bad, was it?"

"No," was the only response I could muster up.

"Are you ready to eat now?" she asked as she got up to move toward the counter.

I shook my head, "Yes, please." She made me a sandwich and gave me cookies and juice as well. While I was eating, I attempted to put my shirt back on.

Quickly she said, "No, don't put that back on. I won't wear my shirt, so you don't need to wear your shirt. It's only right that we're both the same, right?"

"Okay," I replied. After I ate my sandwich, I got up to leave.

"Where are you going without my hug and kiss?" she asked. It was not a peck when I hugged her and kissed her this time. She put her tongue in my mouth, which made my face wet. I remember wiping my mouth. I must admit, although I liked the sandwiches, cookies, and food I would get from her, that kiss made me very scared. I didn't know if I was going to go back. However, my brothers started to catch on to me getting food from over there, and they wanted more also. I had already been taking extra food to them, but it was not close to what I was getting. As much as I did not want to go back, I did not want my brothers to start going over there because I knew what would happen. I returned the next day and asked if I could have a sandwich for them.

"Yes, but you're gonna have to give me a long hug and a better massage next time," she replied. I thought about it for a little bit and agreed. I knew I didn't want to do what she asked of me, but I remember the desperate feeling I had to feed my siblings and the fear that if I did not bring it to them, they would come and ask for it themselves. So, I made up my mind that I would not let them come here and had to do it myself. I did the same routine and massaged her breasts. I gave her a long hug and let her kiss me with wet kiss.

The next time I came over, we did the same routine, but she did not only take our shirts off this time. She made me take my pants off as well. She said she wanted to fight like they do in the cartoons and wrestle around. We began to wrestle, and I only had my underwear on, and she had on her robe. We were wrestling, and I was lying flat on my back while she was hovering over me on her knees. She was holding my hands down as if she was pinning me.

She looked at me and said, "How about I massage you? I will show you how it feels and how it is supposed to be." She began to massage my chest, then kissed me on the stomach. I lay there shocked, scared, and in disbelief. Thinking to myself, no way I will do this same thing to her. I thought I should scream right now, but I felt stuck. I was committed to ensuring I had food for myself and my siblings. My mind quickly snapped back into the moment because she pulled my underwear down and kissed me on my penis.

"What are you doing?" I asked as I jumped up and scooted as far back on the bed as I could go.

She laughed, "Nothing, I'm just giving you a massage." I was looking for a way out, but then I thought of the food.

As an excuse to get away from there, I asked, "Can I have sandwiches for my brothers?"

"Will you come back after taking their food," she asked. I knew then I never wanted to come back. I don't know why I said yes, but I thought that's what I had to say so that I could leave. She got up, made lots of sandwiches, and gave them to me with some other snacks. I did not go back to her room that same day. I was afraid and did not know what would happen next time. What would she ask me to do next? What would she try to do to me next? My mind was racing. Would anyone even believe me if I told them? Would we be kicked out of the motel?

The following day my brothers asked me if I would go to get more food, so I did. I felt like I had to let her do what she wanted to get the food, not just to feed myself but, more importantly, to provide for my siblings.

Once again, I was back in the room that smelled, with the loud TV and dim lighting. I told her that my brothers liked all the food and snacks she gave us. She told me, "If you let me give you a massage for five minutes, I'll give you all the food you want. Your siblings will be thrilled." I could not turn that down because I knew my brothers and sister needed the food. "Take your shirt and pants off," she demanded.

I did as I was told and sat on the bed with my knees folded and pulled up to my chest, arms wrapped around my legs. I was shivering from the cold, and I was very confused. I was scared because I didn't know what was going to happen. I didn't know if she would kiss me down there again or if it would be worse this time. She was more to the point and skipped wrestling, going right to the massage. She told me to lay on my back while she rubbed my arms and shoulders. She massaged my chest and legs for a bit, and then it happened. She pulled down my underwear, kissed me down there a few times, and then put me inside her mouth. I tried to stay there and let her do it for the whole five minutes, but I couldn't. I was naked, cold, and absolutely terrified. I didn't know what to do or what to say.

"Please stop; I am really hungry," I begged. "Will you still give me food if I stop?"

"Yes," she replied sternly. "I will give you everything today and tomorrow as long as you don't tell anyone about our wrestling or massages." I agreed, it was too much food to turn down, so I took the food, and when I returned to my siblings, they were so excited. We had sandwiches, cookies, candy, and juice. They thanked me, and it made me feel good to protect and provide for them.

I knew the way they looked up to me was something special. But it was at the cost that came as I got older when I realized what happened to me. I learned how this lady took advantage of me and sexually abused me repeatedly. I truly believe if we were not taken away by the police because we had been left at the motel alone, the situation would have gone on longer and may have gotten worse.

I did not understand that then, and I still did not understand it in my teenage years. I started to think this was just the right of passage for young boys, and everyone must go through it. I was scared while it was happening, but I didn't know any better. I didn't see it as wrong because an adult was telling me to do it, and I was getting a feast of rewards for it. I guess that's why I never told anyone.

Being sexually abused at such a young age can cause you to alter the way you think about the actual act of sex. Do I think it impacted how soon I became sexually active? Yes, I do believe it did. These things happen far too often in all socioeconomic levels of life, but I believe it is worse in impoverished communities where children can easily be bribed.

I remember the days I would go to school after this experience, and I could never concentrate. I didn't want to be touched or hugged by a teacher or anyone else, and now I realize that was a direct link to the abuse I suffered. I remember some days I would stay quiet, not wanting to talk and not getting close to anyone. I didn't know at the time that being sexually abused was a significant reason, but I was always on edge.

I remember trying to come up with ways to make it stop, but every time I did, I was reminded of the happiness of my siblings when I would bring them the food. As a result, I did as she asked each time to receive my reward. How was a 7-year-old child supposed to make these decisions?

Unfortunately, I found myself in an even worse situation in foster care. I believe the undesirable environments of foster care both helped and hurt me. It brought the animal out of me more than ever before. The primal instinct to survive at all costs was born, and with that, I learned to welcome the animal side—Sudden Death Jr.

It is critical to understand the importance of telling someone you trust if you have been or are being sexually abused. Male or female, embarrassment and self-blame are natural reactions. However, there are people available to get you the help you need. I cannot stress enough how important it is to tell someone. Your safety and mental health depend on finding a teacher or trusted adult to tell.

The damage from this type of abuse is detrimental.

A young me dreaming.

CHAPTER 7 | FOSTER CARELESS

With a quick knock at the door, everything was about to change. I was sitting in our motel room on the floor watching cartoons when I heard a knock at the door. I hesitated for a second, thinking who it could be and if I should answer it. More knocking, I walk to the door, thinking about who it could be? I was scared that it might be the lady from the front office. I opened the door, and to my surprise, it was the police, standing tall like superman, with a strong face and muscular.

I was initially scared, but with a kind smirk and friendly question, he eased my fears. I thought, did I do something wrong? Is someone hurt? Am I in trouble? Then the policeman asked me where my parents were. I told him they were not here. He stepped away and started talking to someone on his radio. A hundred things were going through my mind.

After he got off his radio, he walked back over and asked who was here with me. I said just my sister and brothers, but they are playing outside. He asked me to get them, so I did. We returned to the room where the policeman was still waiting for us. My siblings went into the room, sat on the bed, and started crying instantly. I was standing next to the bed, wondering what he would do with us. We didn't have cell phones back then, so I could not call anyone for help. We could not get in contact with our mother or father.

Since I was only seven, I had not yet realized that we were being taken away from my mom. I was finally out of the motel and the clutches of a grown woman taking advantage of a poor and hungry child. I remember being very happy getting out of there, even though, at that age, I did not realize the severity of the abuse. I did know that they took us away because we were left alone, but I also thought my mom would be able to come to pick us up that same night or the next day. That was not the case.

I recently found out that my mom and aunt took turns checking in to ensure the kids were safe. My aunt was supposed to come by and check on us but had forgotten on this day. There was a miscommunication, and both had decided to do their own thing and hang out this day. Because of this, someone from the hotel called the police to report us being left alone.

We were taken away from the motel and had no idea where we were going or if we would be back. The police officer was very nice on the trip. He even stopped and bought us, Burger King. At this point, I remember having a good feeling about this police officer. How he spoke to me and handled us made it seem like he felt sorry for us. He was a kind man and his actions that day made me think about being a police officer. I was young and had no negative experiences or harsh stories about police officers yet, so I looked up to them. And his generosity added to that feeling. It's funny, but that's all I remember about that ride other than it being long. It had to be within the Chicago area, but I was unsure where.

When we left, it was daytime, and we arrived at our destination at night. We finally pulled in front of a brick house as we stopped. We got out of the car, and a lady who worked with child services was there waiting for us. We all walked towards the front door, and once we reached the door, the lady knocked. The anticipation for someone to come to the door felt like forever. I did not know what to think or how to feel. Neither of them told us anything. All I remember was my older sister and two younger brothers standing there holding my hands. I could feel them squeezing and pulling on me. I tried to stand tall and strong, but I may have been more scared than they were. I wanted to cry because I knew things were about to get weird. I did not know what to expect, but I knew it would not be anything that we were used to.

The door swung open, and a sudden gust of air hit our face. The air was saturated with the smell of poop, mothballs, feet, and medicine. An older man in a wheelchair was staring at us face to face. The only emotions that I can remember are fear and anger. I was so angry that they would bring us here. The sheer smell of the place made me want to turn and run. Seconds after the old man appeared, he was joined by an older lady. She came with a big fake smile that I could read from a mile away, and I could tell this was about to be our new hell.

They were putting on an excellent show for the police officer and this social worker. From what I could gather, it seemed like we were about to live at this home for now. When I figured that out, I yelled, "We're not fucking staying here." The policeman looked at me as if I had said something wrong. But I did not care, and I yelled again, "Fuck that!" Again, a glance from the police officer would reveal disappointment because of the language I had started to use.

The social worker tried asking me to calm down, telling me that everything would be ok and we would only be there for a little while. I was devastated because my sister and brothers standing behind me started crying because of the commotion I had created. The old lady in the house started talking to my brothers to calm them down. Whatever she was saying, it was working for them. But it was not working for my sister Tasha or me. Tasha was the fighter when we were younger, and we both could see past those fake words.

My grandma, Lil Freddie, always used to say that I could see the truth in people. As I got older, we would talk about what that meant. She would say that God gave me the blessing of identifying good people and their truths. I never really understood this until I became closer to my spirituality. My grandma used to say once that closeness happened, only then would I know and understand the gift that I had been entrusted with. She was 100% correct, and this particular gift has allowed me to connect with my students, players, those I have coached, and those I've managed.

The police officer and social worker ushered us into the house. I truly believe the police officer wanted to do more for us, but he could not. As much as I fought it, there was nothing I could do. One minute everyone is talking and saying nice things to make us feel better about being here, and the next minute I turn around, the officer and social worker are gone. They just left us in this nasty living room with all these other kids running around all over the place!

The house was older and filled with clutter. The furniture had plastic on it, and there were a lot of pictures of old people hanging on the walls and a lot of doors. There were dusty flowers and old dolls everywhere.

The old man was in a wheelchair when he did not wear his fake leg. He started to talk to us. He said I would stay upstairs with the older boys, my sister upstairs with the older girls, and my two younger brothers would stay downstairs with the younger kids. This separation brought tears all over again, but they were screaming and terrified this time. It was a gut-wrenching type of crying that would make a stranger who did not know what was going on cry along with them. It broke my heart, and even at such a young age, I remember feeling like I had failed them again. How the hell was I going to protect them and take care of them from upstairs. There were so many things running through my head.

To make things worse, that old man who acted so nice when the policeman and social worker were there looked over at them with an ugly face and yelled, "Stop all that fucking crying before I beat ya'll ass!" I looked at this man and went crazy. I started swinging and kicking, trying my hardest to get to this jerk who had just threatened my siblings. We had not been there longer than thirty minutes, and already I was in fear for their safety.

The old lady aggressively walked my sister and me up the stairs while pulling me by my arm with one hand and maintaining her tight grip around my neck with her other. as she guided me. Once up the stairs, the old lady pointed to a room and told my sister to go in.

During my interviews for this book, my sister stated when it was time for her to be separated from me, she felt scared and did not know what would happen to her. Even as an adult, hearing this broke my heart. The burden of protecting those in my life has always weighed heavy on me.

I was mad and wanted to burn the whole house down on the first day. I was in a rage and could not get a hold of myself. Like many times when I was younger, my anger would make me cry. I do not know why that was my body's reaction, but everyone knew that if I started to cry, that meant I was about to explode!

While upstairs, the woman of the house showed me where I would be sleeping and walked away. She soon returned with a few pairs of socks, t-shirts, and other items. She handed them to me and walked away, shaking her head. I guess in disbelief that I was acting the way I was. Once she left, I took my stuff and climbed into the bed.

I took one of the t-shirts and stuffed everything else in it. Stuffing everything in the t-shirt would do two things for me. It would allow all of my items to be in one spot, making it easier to watch and ensuring no one could steal them. But it also would serve as a pillow. I had what seemed like a comfortable bed, but it had no sheets, pillow, or anything to cover myself with while I slept.

Once everything was stuffed in my t-shirt, I threw it towards the top of the bed and plopped down on it. I could feel all the lumps as I lay there trying to calm down.

I could do nothing but think about my brothers and sister. Who would take care of them? Who would protect them? It was an awful feeling, and there was nothing I could do about it. I felt like I was born to be a protector by any means necessary. This would be a pivotal feeling that often showed its face in my life.

A few days had passed, and I could finally see them. My little brothers asked why they could not come upstairs with me, and I had to tell them it was because they were younger, and it was all older and bigger kids upstairs. As much as I hated being separated, I was thankful they did not have to be up there after seeing what it was like in those first days.

The second day I was there, I found myself in the crosshairs of a group of older boys who had been there for a while.

One boy had it out for me. I assume it was just part of being the new kid. The second day, he and some boy walked over to my bed and asked for one of my t-shirts. I did not want to give it to him because the foster mother told me those would be the only ones I would get, so I better take care of them. He asked for the t-shirt again.

I positioned myself between him and my bed, where my makeshift pillow filled with my things was at the time. I again told him no. He turned around and looked at the other kids because they were teasing him since I had told him no twice. As I looked at the boys laughing at him, he made a streetfighter-type spin move that made his body face me again. I did not see his fist with him until it connected to my face with the force of a freight train. I was down, and just like that, both of my t-shirts were gone. My lips were busted, and blood was coming down my mouth. I stood up as they walked away, laughing at how hard I had fallen.

I was angry, but not mad enough to fight back, at least not yet. I got on my bed and just sat there, thinking about what I should do about it. The kids were bigger than I was, but I could not let him get away with this. If I did, he would come back to take more. I was nervous and scared they would come back the whole day, but they never did. The day would end, and I don't think I ever got off the bed besides going to the bathroom.

The night came, and I was still mad. I was out of two t-shirts, sporting a pair of freshly busted lips, and a dish of embarrassment for getting punched in the face. As night came over the whole house, everyone started to take their usual spots in their beds.

While I sat on my bed and plotted how I would make him pay for what he had done to me earlier, once everyone was asleep, I got out of the bed and quietly went over to the bully's bed. I first went into his bag, took the only t-shirt I could find, and hurried over to put it back with my stuff.

At first, all I wanted to do was get my shirts back, but I got so angry. I was mad because he was sleeping so well, and I was stressed the whole night. I felt that I had to make him pay. The problem was that I knew I could not beat this kid in a one-on-one fight. Not a fair fight anyway. So, whatever I did, I would have to accept the consequences of my actions. I thought about what would make me happy. I had to be able to wake up the next morning feeling good about myself. I concluded that I just wanted to hit this dirtbag as hard as possible! That one act would make me feel amazing. I wanted to embarrass him the same way I was embarrassed the whole day.

I woke the two boys that were next to me. These two had told me to leave him alone and not do anything back, or he would keep picking on me. I woke them up because I needed someone to witness this epic battle. I was going to punch him with all my might and make his face bleed as mine did.

They sat up quietly, watching me closely. One shook his head in disbelief. The other looked concerned with his hand over his mouth and shaking his head to tell me not to go through it. I look back one last time to make sure that they are still watching, and one now had a smile on his face with a sign of glee. He was excited and ready for this to go down.

As I stood on the side of this kid's bed, other boys in the home started to wake up, and they started making noise as the other two boys were trying to get them to hush. I look back to get everyone to shut up, and out of nowhere, the boy whose bed I am standing in front of starts to sit up, and I thought he was about to ask me something. But as the words started to come out of his mouth, I pulled my arm back as far as I could, gathering all my anger from earlier in the day to turn into strength. My arm is now in motion towards his face, but my fist chickened out and opened up. I am now in full open-hand slap motion. But before I could think of anything else, my open hand connected to the side of this boy's face.

It seemed like everything was in slow motion. I could see his cheek and lips moving from the power of the slap. I was excited, and I couldn't wait to see the blood. Before I could turn to celebrate my epic slap, he jumped out of his bed and landed right in front of me. I looked at him and thought I was about to say something slick. But before I could get words out of my mouth, he had hit me back-to-back more times than I could count.

Everyone was trying to pull him off of me, but they were stepping on me while they were doing it. They were hurting me more than helping me. The only reason he did not beat me to death is that the foster parents came into the room because of all the noise, and they broke everything up. I made it back to my bed, and I had knots all over my head and body. But for some reason, the only thing I could think of was how hard I had slapped this bully. I was proud of myself!

After waking up the next day, I thought everyone would make fun of me again for getting beat up. To my surprise, the talk leaned in favor of my epic slap more than the butt whooping I took following the slap. I think most of them had wanted to slap this kid like that. Although these boys still didn't like me, not many would pick with me because they knew if I had to get them back, I would do it while they were sleeping.

I learned a valuable lesson from that situation. What I learned would stick with me throughout my life. I have always believed that standing up to a bully is always the better option. I took on anyone who wanted to fight me from that point on. I did not win all my battles, but I had gotten so used to being punched that it did not hurt that much anymore, and honestly, I thrived in that feeling of aggression.

I had gotten pretty good at fighting because I had done it so much. When I did get into fights, I always thought it was a good idea to go to the extreme because it would make other people not want to fight me. Because I was a small kid, I would have to go to the extreme often. As I got older, I often wondered if that thrilling feeling of aggression was how my mother could deal with the traumatic abuse she had dealt with for years from the hands of different men, even though she could never win.

Although the fight with this bully was my fault, I thought both of us should have gotten in trouble because he took my t-shirts and what he did after I slapped him. Our foster parents did not see it that way, and I suffered the bulk of the punishments while at this foster home. This time my punishment would be a beating from the foster dad of the house. I had gotten used to being abused, but they started to get worse because of my history of running around the room trying to escape the beatings. Because the foster dad could not move well, he would often tie me to the bedpost so I could not run away.

After this beating, the foster mom entered the room, untied me, and took me downstairs to the basement. She said since I could not get along with the other boys, I should spend some time alone in the basement. I would get sent to the basement all the time. They never wanted to hear my side of the story. Any problems were always my fault, no matter who started them.

It was a dark and damp basement, all concrete, not the finished basements we see today. It had spider webs,

69

bugs, and dripping water. Sometimes the foster mother would tie me to the pole so I would not keep coming to the door asking if I could come out. She took the light bulb out so I could not turn the light on, leaving me to count on a sunny day as my only hope for light during the day, and the nights were pitch black. That fight caused me to be down there for almost three days. Three long days tied to the pole alone. I learned to live within my mind during these times.

In hard times I think back to the days in the basement, and I tell myself at least it's not as bad as being tied to a pole in a dark, scary basement. To this day, it doesn't matter what the situation is; I always decide in my mind that everything will be ok. Even when I am going through a rough situation, I am grateful that it is not as bad as it could be. Even though people around me may panic and think that my problem is pretty bad, I maintain my composure and do not complain. While spending those days in the basement, I learned that I control how I feel. If I can manage my thoughts, then I ultimately control what my reactions will be.

When I lose my temper, it is because I choose to. If I think the situation calls for me to turn up my temperature, I do. When the situation calls for me to turn it down, that is what I do. But I am the one who decides when I will make those adjustments. I am stronger than anything that anyone can ever throw at me. So I make the mental adjustments, and I deal with and accept what comes with the adjustments.

While in this foster home, I learned how much adults could hate children. As I have grown, I've heard many stories from other children that lived in foster homes. The horror stories continue to break my heart. I have never understood the motivation for adults to treat children in such horrible ways when they have agreed to take the children into their homes. Yes, most are motivated by money, but I also believe some need someone to mistreat, so they take on vulnerable children.

Many foster children speak about the mental, physical, and sexual abuse within this system. What can be done is a frequent thought that I wrestle with. Wishing I could discover the answer, I sit with grief, knowing what goes on behind these smiling faces.

I always thought that being an adult meant you were obligated to do right by children. But that was not the case, and I learned that based on the actions of my foster parents. I hate even giving them this much attention, but their actions and treatment of me had such a lasting impact on my life that I feel I must share it. I think these stories can help other adults understand how their actions can affect the children in their care.

My foster dad called me down one morning to ask me to help him put his leg on. I handed him the leg, but I would not help him attach it, which made him furious. He called me a few names and told me to get back upstairs. I tried to tell him everyone was downstairs getting ready to play, but he did not care. He called me dirty and yelled at me to go back upstairs. I stood there for a short time in disbelief. At that moment, my mind was scrambled and honestly tired of so much abuse it made me freeze. I was not trying to be disrespectful, but I felt like I had zoned out. I had not moved or moved fast enough. I could not hear or see anything, and I had no idea he was moving toward me. The sting of his hand on my face made me snap out of it. He slapped me so hard that my ear rang for a few days afterward.

I moved as fast as I could and ran up the stairs. I spent the whole day up there and did not get to play with the other kids on this fun day. I was sad, but it made me more angry than hurt.

Often, I was ganged up on and could not battle everyone at once, so I would find myself waiting until I could catch some of them by themselves before retaliating. While moving around the house, I saw one of the boys that had earlier been a part of a group of boys who were ganging up on me. He was one of the boys who helped hold me down while the other boys put the foster mom's dirty panties in my face. I saw him walking alone while I was sweeping the floor, and it set me off. So, I ran up to him and hit him across his head and back with the broom. I know this was wrong, but I felt this was an opportunity I had to take because I had to let them know what would happen to them if they tried to bully me.

During this fight, the foster mom came and grabbed me off the other boy by my shirt so hard I could feel the pressure around the front of my neck. She started yelling at me, asking why I was always starting trouble. Hearing the commotion, the foster dad came out. They both were shouting and calling me names simultaneously, and the whole time I was standing there trying to block it out. My adrenaline was pumping, and I was ready for anything, so I thought. The foster mom grabbed me by the neck and took me into a room with two sets of bunk beds and nothing else in the room. It was cold, with wood flooring and ugly curtains.

Once we were in the room, she told me to take my pants off. I was mad because I knew what was about to happen. But I never understood why the other kids never got a beating when they would do something to me. Maybe it was because they had been there longer. She beat me with a belt, but I made her work for it. I was running all over that room, and she was moving just as quickly, trying to grab me. I tried to get out of the door, and she slammed the door shut. The problem was that my hand had been in the way. Now, I had a hurt body and a smashed hand. The door made one of the nails on my hand turn purple and swell up. I quickly hit the floor and held on to my smashed hand. The pain from the door was ten times worse than the pain from the many hits of the belt.

As I lay on the cold floor, she beat my body for as long as she could with the belt. I stared at those ugly curtains wondering if this was life. Wondering how long I could take this. Why was I so hated at such a young age? What did I do to deserve this?

Years later, my sister spoke out about being sexually abused by the foster dad many times. After hearing that from her, I was heartbroken and disappointed in myself for not helping her. Again, I could not protect another person in my life, which hurt my heart.

In my early life, I experienced many situations involving people I could not protect, and they would haunt me throughout my life. These situations would become the driving force of motivation for much-needed healing. I wanted to make up for all the times I could not protect the people I loved. I wanted to find those who hurt my family and friends and make them pay somehow, to make them as scared and uncomfortable as they made the people I loved. This obsession got worse as it moved from wanting to protect those I love to the need to protect everyone. I dated a woman who told me about a boyfriend who had done some things to her that were not right. It had damaged her for a long time, and I wanted to go and find him and hurt him.

During the week leading up to my grandmother Lil Freddie's funeral, her oldest son told me the truth about how my grandfather had treated her in their early years together. She was truly like a second mother to me and often the source of my motivation and support. My uncle told me some things my grandfather did to hurt her, which made me furious. But unfortunately, we had lost him just two years before losing her.

At his funeral, I spoke highly of him because I try to find the good in most people. I think it helps that I am a man of many flaws. Because of this, I can see and understand how the power of personal growth changes many.

This feeling is the best way to explain the hurt that I experienced while not being able to be there for my siblings during this time of our lives. The short time at that foster home made me more rigid than I wanted to be at that age. I wanted to be a kid, but I could not. I wanted to feel protected, but I did not. I was not safe and moved throughout my days, always on edge. I do not know if I was scared or just always alert. I experienced a lot of physical abuse at this group home, but the mental abuse hurt me more. Over and over, I would wonder why life was like this for my siblings and me. I would find myself thinking if other children were living the same way. I wondered if this was all I had to look forward to for the rest of my life.

Sister Tasha and brother Wayne

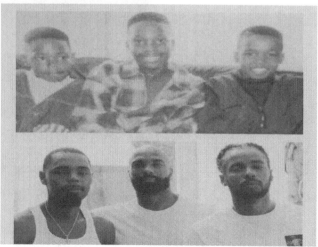

Then and Now pictures of Wayne, Me, and Taiwan

CHAPTER 8 | MOTHER TO THE RESCUE

Just like that, I was eight years old, but finally, it was time for us to leave this horrible place of a foster home. Dropped off by a policeman and social worker and left to survive on our own with no support and no check-ins to see how we were adjusting to the new environment. Finally, it was over. My mom went through a lot to finally get us back, she had secured a home for us all to live in, and there was no one there to mistreat us. At least not like at the foster home.

I can honestly say that I had never really looked at my mother in a negative light because of what we went through. I was often angry and hurt, but for some reason, I continued to think that she was doing the best she knew how to do. I was self-aware enough at a young age to understand that some of my actions contributed to how I was being treated. The situations we were in made me mad, and I wished things were better, but I can't say I blamed her. I was just so happy to be back with her that I overlooked a lot of what we did not have or the wrong ways we were treated. I loved my mother, and sometimes I felt just as bad for her as I did for us. I love her for putting forth the effort to get us back. Maybe it is because of what my grandmother, Lil Freddie, used to say about me. "Boy, you always see the good in people."

As much turmoil as we had while living with our mom and sometimes father, we were much happier being with them than in that horrible foster home. We spent so much time playing with each other and running around. We had a ball at this new place, we made up all types of games, and because there were so many of us, we always had someone to play with.

We did not have many material things, but we laughed together, and that was enough. We learned to enjoy each other's company and even found joy in going to school, which we had never done before. We were still being bullied for not having nice clothes and shoes, but we were getting by. Our clothing was not just cheap, but they were hand-me-downs or things we had found. Even if things were not perfect, we were so happy to be back together and with our mother. However, this fun would only last for a short time because a new boyfriend of my mom's came along quickly.

PART 2

JOLIET JOURNEY

CHAPTER 9 | MOVE AND MOVE AGAIN

Shortly after my mom and dad separated for good, my mom met a man named Joe and started dating him. He was a smooth-talking, smooth-dressing drug dealer who was an absolute jerk. I remember how he would wake up first thing in the morning and iron a crease in his pants that would last for days.

Because she was dating Joe, we moved from Summit to Joliet, Illinois. It is about 40 minutes outside Chicago, but it was still a rough neighborhood. I remember my dad finding out about this new man, and he wasn't happy about it. He beat my mom up and gave her a black eye because she had decided to leave him. I remember feeling helpless watching, even though, yet again, I wanted to be her hero and save her from him.

This move to Joliet sucked, as we lived in and out of motels for months at a time. My mom and her new jerk of a boyfriend would wake up, shower, get dressed, and hit the streets while leaving me, two of my brothers, and my older sister at the motel the whole day and night.

Most of the time, we would not have food to eat. So, we would make our way across the street to a gas station or grocery store. We would steal as much candy and food as we could hide in our pockets, coats, or armpits.

My brother Taiwan and I would grab our coats and do a little shopping. Because we were so young, we did not understand some of the signs that store managers would notice when people were coming into the store to steal. But we came to find out that one of those tell-tale signs was wearing a winter coat inside a store when it was 98 degrees during a Chicago summer.

Taiwan is the brother that falls underneath me age-wise. He is the third oldest of the children. He was the perfect brother to take with me for this job because he was fearless. As we got older, it would turn out that Taiwan would be the ideal brother to take for any job because he was fearless and tough at a young age. He would repeatedly prove that he could fight and win against anyone. He made a name for himself, just like our father, 'Sudden Death.'

Taiwan and I headed across the street to Jewel's grocery store, which was a popular chain in the Midwest. We started to shop for our regular items, candy, cupcakes, bread, and lunch meat. We were doing great like always, so we thought. But there was one problem. Someone had caught on to what we were doing because we had on our oversized winter coats, and it was super hot out that day. As soon as we walked in, we stuck out like two sore thumbs. They were on to us right away, and they followed us the entire time. Once we finished shopping, we headed to the door as quickly as possible. We got to the door, and we heard the manager yell, "Hey!"

I knew right away that it was over. I took off running with Taiwan right behind me. We made a break for the parking lot and then had to swerve not to get hit by a car backing out. We reached the main street and could see our motel in the distance. The manager and security guard were not far behind us. I could see them running at full speed to catch up. But we could not cross the street because there was too much traffic. Taiwan said, "Fuck this," and started to run through the traffic. I took off right behind him, dodging cars as we weaved in and out of the oncoming traffic.

We both made it safely across to the motel, but the manager and security guard had seen where we had run. We returned to the room and started telling our other brother and sister what had just happened, and they laughed at us. We were sitting there looking at all the great food from the store, feeling happy that we had gotten away and excited that we were about to eat well.

Then, suddenly, a knock at the door. Everyone sat quietly, but I am sure whoever was knocking had already heard us and knew we were in there. A stern voice said, "Open up, guys; we are going to unlock the door." We still did not open it, but sure enough, they did what they said and opened the door themselves. It was the motel manager, the store manager, and the police.

We were busted, sitting there eating all the food we had just stolen from the store. The manager took us back to the store, where he wrote a report and took our names. Luckily the store didn't press it any further than that.

Some were awful, but we had many good days together at the motels. The only thing we wanted was not to get beat, to stay at a decent motel with a working TV, and to have a little food we could eat. We were not hard to please, so if we could fulfil those needs, we would be fine with everything else.

My brother Taiwan aka "Can't Get Right"

CHAPTER 10 | SAME CLOTHES

I was still eight years old, and we had yet another move within the city of Joliet. This time it was to a little garage that someone turned into a one-room apartment. It was unique because there was one big room and a bathroom. That meant we were all together the whole day.

We never met the people that lived in the actual house, but when we would leave in the morning to head to school, I could smell breakfast sometimes. I have to admit that made me jealous because most mornings, we would not eat until we got to school.

Through moments like these, I remember thinking to myself that I would make sure my children always had breakfast before they left in the mornings.

My growth was strange and spontaneous; I had no clue what was expected of me. I had no idea how to navigate my life and all the ups and downs I faced daily. It was a pure guessing game while trapped playing Russian roulette with a life that already had many strikes against it. But here I was.

I could not have and did not make it through all these shortcomings on my own. Teachers have always played a massive part in my life. Often for the better but sometimes for worse.

As a little boy, I had been let down by so many people so early in life that it just became my expectation to be disappointed. I did not trust anyone and was past the point of caring for help. I had grown to hate anyone who was an authority figure because, in my eyes, an adult in the position of authority should have been the person to save us. In America, children of all races are mistreated, but the plight of the little black boy is an unmatched struggle. I knew other children were going through similar experiences as my siblings and me, but it seemed as if we always had it the worst. It seemed like we had the worst shoes, haircut (if any), and our clothes were always the smallest. We never had school supplies or lunch money and seemed to stick out more than any of the other poor kids.

There were obvious things brought to the forefront of everyone's eyesight when it came to us. But the one thing I know for sure is that you never know what is going on behind the closed doors of someone else's home. How big does the obvious burden have to be for an adult to recognize that a child is struggling?

I wore the same clothes to school at least three times a week. We did not brush our teeth often or wear deodorant. Even when I took baths, I wore the same socks and shoes so much that my feet would smell horrendous. We did not have easy access to washing our clothes, so sometimes, we would use dish detergent to wash them out by hand in the sink or tub. My favorite pants were high-rising, blue pants that were way too tight and usually filthy. I recall having a rough time at school because I had fallen behind so much and felt like I was just not smart enough to keep up.

As a result, I got picked on and bullied during class and outside at recess. The kids would make fun of me, throw stuff at me, and want to fight regularly. Because this would happen so much, I would always get mad and stand against the wall or next to the swing set that no other students occupied.

One day I'd had enough, so I approached the teacher to tell her what was happening. I told her some kids had been picking on me, bullying me, and making fun of me. She then looked at a teacher standing next to her and laughed. "I'm sure no one is making fun of you," she said, then told me to go play and that it would be ok. At this point, I knew it made no sense to ask for help from this teacher.

While sitting in class going through the day's lesson, a kid told me that my feet smelled bad, and the kids that heard him started to laugh. I got angry, and I was very hurt. I felt the tears beginning to come, but I didn't want anyone to know that I was going to cry, so I yelled out, "Fuck you, you stupid bitch!"

Those are the only curse words I could put together to express my anger. The student said something back to me, and as soon as he did, I punched him as hard as possible. Only then did the teacher come over to separate us. I started to swing, yell, curse, kick, scratch, and do everything else I could think of. I wanted to get my hands on that kid and the teacher's hands off me. I even started to yell at her. I was calling her names and cursing at her. I told her how much I hated her.

Did I hate her? No. But I distrusted her because she did nothing to help me after I told her I was being bullied. I did not feel protected since I had told her about these kids picking on me, but she did not help or even acknowledge it was happening.

After that incident, I did not like that teacher. I saw her as one of the bullies and many people who did not love me. In my mind, she did not care about me enough to help when I asked for it. After the fight, the teacher took me to the principal's office, and she told the principal that I had hit another kid. I got paddled, and the principal sent me back to class. I no longer wanted to be in this class at that point.

This situation stands out in my mind because it's honestly the first time I remember thinking I did not want to be alive anymore. I didn't want to be at school and thought I would be better off dead. Had that teacher tried to see what was happening and helped me, I would have started to build trust with her and not just lash out. Even seemingly small bullying situations can make a child with a difficult home life have suicidal thoughts.

Most teachers fail to realize the impact of a child's negative home life or its role on a student's ability to get along with other kids and focus while at school—the few educators who understand this may not know how to handle the student struggling with home-life barriers.

The following day, I returned to class with the same pants, shoes, socks, and shirt I had on the day before. I don't even remember if I had a bath that night. During the walk to school, I knew what I was in for. I knew the kids would make fun of me and call me names, and I knew the teacher wouldn't stop them. There was no way I could have focused on anything educational after enduring daily bullying and the other students staring at me. The teacher was also staring at me, and I could see the disgust on her face. I had made it through the day without getting into any fights, even though I could have punched at least three kids. As I walked towards the door to leave, the teacher called my name. As I approached her, I could see she held a folded-up sheet of paper. She stuffed the paper in an envelope and asked me to give it to my mother. When I got home, I gave the letter to my mother.

I could tell it was not good because of how she looked up at me. My mom's nose scrunched up, and she bit down hard on her teeth. I had no idea what the letter said, but she called me closer to her. She said, "I don't give a crap what your teacher says. Tell that bitch if she has a problem with you wearing the same clothes to school, she should buy you some new ones." After my mom finished swearing at me and being upset, she realized I could not say those words to the teacher. So, she wrote a reply letter saying everything she had previously told me to say. After she calmed down, she called me into her room and said that I better not tell those teachers anything about this house. As I was standing there getting chewed out, the only thing I could think was that I did not have to tell the teachers at the school anything. They can see and smell what is going on with me.

As I was walking to school the following day, I must have lost the letter because I could not find it. I was not going to say anything to my teacher because I was embarrassed. The teacher called me up to the front of the classroom and asked me about the letter she had sent home with me. I told the teacher that I had lost it. Her response was very mean, and she asked me why I was so irresponsible. Being blamed made me angry, so I thought about the letter and what my mom told me to say. Since the teacher had been so rude about it, I did not hold back.

I yelled out, "My mom said she didn't give a shit what you thought, you stupid bitch! And if you don't like my clothes, you should buy me some yourself!" As I turned to walk to my seat, she got up from her desk, grabbed my arm, walked me outside the classroom, and made me stand in the hallway. With that, she only added more embarrassment to my day. She was unhappy with the language I had used and did not allow me back until after lunch.

After letting me back into the classroom, she made me stand in the corner, adding to my full day of embarrassment. I was so desperate to get out of that corner that I stuck my fingers down my throat and made myself throw up all over the wall. It splashed all over the place, and there was no more standing in the corner for me that day.

Looking back on it, I'm unsure if that teacher understood the pain she had caused me. Maybe she did not realize that for a young boy to snitch on another student was a big step, and it was my cry for help. Since she had written me off as just a bad kid and laughed at my outward cry for help, she broke the thread of the possibility I would ever trust her.

That teacher had an opening, and she did not see it or care enough to try to use that opening to make a difference. In that first moment when I told her of the bullying, she could have sat me down to kindly explain that smelling and having dirty clothes could lead to kids picking on me, and she would try to intervene when that happened. She could have seen my reaction after giving my mom the letter she sent home and realized I may not have had the help or means to change my situation. With the severing of that thread, my pattern of bad behavior towards her and instant anger reactions to my bullies would never be able to change.

So many small instances often go unnoticed or blatantly ignored, but a substantial impact can be made on a struggling child in those tiny openings. Never write off bad behavior as just another bad child. Look deeper into that child's soul and surroundings to see if the behavior stems from a significant need.

Why Me

Why Me

Roses are red

Violets are blue

I like you

I would like you to like me too.

Other teachers like me

Why don't you.

Sorry I smell bad

Sorry I can't spell red

I will try hard in class

Make my grades better

And I will make friends

Why me

Why don't you like me?

—C.Davis

CHAPTER 11 | THE GREAT ESCAPE THAT FAILED

I reached a point where I could not take it anymore and did not want to stay at the motel in Joliet. I was now nine years old, and we had been living in and out of motels for so long that I was ready for a change. If not at a motel, it would be someone else's house for a day or two and then off to a new place.

We would fall asleep anywhere, on the floor, on the couch, or even sitting at a table. Sometimes we would even put together chairs and sleep on them, often never having anything to cover ourselves. It was uncomfortable and exhausting.

I felt like I was wasting my life away and not living. Even as a child, I knew this was no way to live. I had watched my older sister run away from the motel to live with our mother's mom. Tasha had been living the good life, from what we could tell. Everyone called her Lil Freddie, but her grandchildren had also called her 'Mama.'

On this day, I had decided that it was time for me to get out. I told my two brothers that we would have a party and eat everything in the room, and they should tell our mom that I ate it or took it with me. Nothing would be off-limits. Our bellies would be full on this day. While eating, I grabbed the phone in our room to call for a taxi cab.

I had taken the first step to freedom. I would be on my way to living the good life, with food every day, and I would be around people who loved me. They might even tell me they loved me a few times. Once the cab arrived, I hugged my brothers and wished them luck. I felt horrible at the time because I knew I was leaving them in a bad situation.

To this day, I still have not been able to live that down, and I still hold that in my heart. I find myself trying to make up for situations like that one. Leaving them behind scared me. What kind of big brother was I to leave them in conditions that even I wanted to escape? Looking back, I was only thinking about my self-preservation. All I knew for sure was that I no longer wanted to suffer from the trauma I suffered at that time of my life.

It had been about a year since my sister had gotten away, and when we saw her, she was always so happy, clean, and well dressed, and I have to admit she was getting a little chunky. So, we could tell she had been eating well. I wanted to experience that, to taste a piece of that life. So what was I to do? I thought my younger brothers would be better cared for without me.

We ate everything we could reach. I wanted to take the blame since I didn't think my mom would drive to grandma's house to beat me. A knock at the door meant the cab was here. I grabbed the few things I had and walked to the car. It felt like the longest walk of my lifetime. I was terrified that any second while I was leaving the motel, my mom and her boyfriend would catch me trying to escape, even though they had never returned home this early.

I made it from the motel's top floor, down the hallways, through the lobby, and was soon in the cab on my way to glory. It was sunny outside, and I felt free. I felt like I had been locked in prison for years. I was excited but also fearful. As the drive began, I looked at the trees, buildings, and sky. It felt like music waves. The sun was beautiful, like a musical on Broadway. The weight that lifted from my chest was incredible. It was freedom. I had never felt more excited and joyous.

At last, I had arrived at Arizona Street, the white house sitting on top of the hill. I was so excited and felt overwhelmed with joy. I also felt a tinge of disbelief and fear. I was thinking, what if my mom was inside waiting for me. What if my grandma did not want me? Would it just be another heartbreak and disappointment? Another adult in my life who did not want me. But it was time to try. I got out of the car and ran up the driveway to an open door.

My grandmother was just as excited to see me as I was to see her. She hugged me and asked me how I was doing. I told her I was good and had to throw in how happy I was to see her. But then it happened. She paused and finally asked me where everybody else was. I took a breath and told her that Taiwan and Wayne were still at the motel.

"Where is your mom?" she asked.

"I don't know. I came by myself. I took a cab."

"You did what?" was her shocked response.

"I took a cab," I repeated, terrified of the tension of the conversation.

"Where is the cab?" she asked.

"He is outside waiting for you."

"What the hell is he out there waiting for me for?" she responded with vigor. I didn't say anything; I just stood there looking crazy. I was afraid to say anything at all. Then my grandmother took me by the hand and walked outside.

She walked up to the cab driver, and he said, "Are you the one who is going to pay for this boy's fare to get here?"

My grandma looked at me, then at the cab driver, "Hell no, how much is the fare anyway?" Before he could even respond, my grandma said, "I don't have no goddamn money to pay for a taxi!"

"Well, somebody has got to pay for this ride," he replied.

My grandma said sternly, "You are the one who picked him up. You can take his ass back where you got him because I am not paying!"

When my grandma said those infamous words, my face had to have a look of death because that is how I felt inside. The level of heartbreak that engulfed my body at that point is indescribable. I looked up at her with the saddest eyes. I was trying to get my eyes to speak to her. Trying to say, "Please save me because you do not know what you will make me face when I get back. The war I am about to embark on is unwinnable." I could only imagine the beating that would be waiting for me. I honestly thought they would kill me if she made me return to the hotel.

So with my last calm breath, "Grandma, please, please pay for the fare because I cannot go back to the motel."

She looked at me and said, "Baby, I love you, but I do not have money to pay for this. You are going to have to go back." I could feel my soul being snatched out of my body with those words. As I got back into the cab's backseat, I started sweating. Driving back to the motel seemed like the fastest drive I had ever taken. My shirt was wet from the sweat, my legs stiff from the fear of walking back into this warzone. I reached for the door handle to open the car door, but my fingers could not flex correctly to grab hold. I finally got the door open and exited the cab. I stood frozen for a few seconds as I took in the scenery. I look at the sky, the sun, and the buildings around me.

As I looked back at the cab driver, he told me to shut the door. He was mad that he'd wasted his time. He pulled away so fast he nearly burned rubber. I took the same route to get back to our room as I did when escaping. There was no joy, relief, or excitement—none of the same feelings I had just experienced earlier in the day. I knocked, and they would not answer. I had to call out and tell them to open the door. As the door opened, the looks on their faces were the only thing that calmed me down and made me feel better. They were happy to see me but curious about why I had returned.

I told them Grandma said she did not have money to pay for my cab fare. They started to panic, and I could see the fear all over their faces. They were thinking about all the food we had eaten a few hours earlier. I told them my stupid idea did not work, so the new plan was to say I ate everything by myself. Whatever we decided to tell them, I would be the one to take the blame for it all. We tried to make the best out of the situation and focus on having fun like we usually did when left in the room all day. All I had on my mind was how this would be my last night on earth. We ended the night watching TV and finally falling asleep.

My mom and her boyfriend returned to the room in the middle of the night. Once they went to bed, I finally fell back asleep. The following day came, and they got up and started preparing to leave for the day. They had not said anything about the missing food. Did they not care? Had they expected this type of thing to happen sooner or later? Or maybe they honestly did not notice yet.

But my mom was a professional detective, one of the best. She could tell when something was out of place or missing. She could look at our faces and know when we had done something wrong, and I knew she had this particular superpower. That is why I pretended I was asleep for the whole morning. I planned to pretend I was sleeping until they left. As they are getting ready to go, I felt like I had gotten away with the mess-up of the year.

They both were dressed and smelling good, getting ready to walk out of the door, and the phone rang.

My mom's boyfriend answered the phone, and I heard him say, "Yeah, okay, who?"

"Went where?"

"Okay, thank you," and he hung up the phone. I could feel him staring at me, but I kept my eyes closed and pretended I was still sleeping. He called my mom back into the room and said, "One of your kids took a cab to Arizona Street."

The time had come for me to die. When I heard this, I started crying inside. My mom looked at all three of us and yelled, "Wake y'all asses up. Which one of y'all took a cab?"

As hard as it was, I spoke up quickly to ensure my brothers did not get in trouble. I said it was me, then told her I had eaten all the food before leaving. She then ripped all the blankets, pillows everything off the bed we were lying on. She told me to take all my clothes off, down to my underwear.

She grabbed the cord from the telephone in the room and started to whip me with it. I do not know if she was madder at me for eating all the food, the cost of the cab, or that I tried to leave her to live with my grandmother. I am not sure, but either way, I got my butt beat, and after they left, we continued on the same circle of daily life.

It was undoubtedly a debacle of a runaway attempt. I learned many things from this event, but the bright side was we had an open buffet for a day. However, the biggest downside was that I had gained another notch of rejection from another person in my life. But that rejection helped me to build strength. I believe it gave me the motivation to hunt for acceptance and the ability to get the results I wanted. It opened my eyes and my imagination to find a way.

I adopted the practice of examining all my failures and preparing myself to prevent them from happening again. I would use these rejections to test how I would handle letdowns in my life. Would I fold because I had not achieved the results I set out to accomplish on my first attempt? Or would I get back up and swing again, this time being better prepared and learning from the failed attempt? I would use and apply this reevaluation and retry principle throughout my life. Giving up would never be an option for me. And it should never be an option for you.

Dancing with my grandmother "Lil Freddie"

CHAPTER 12 | MY FIRST DRIVE BY

I remember it like it was yesterday, another decent day in Joliet. I was nine years old and outside playing with two of my friends, Benjamin and William. We met at the beginning of the school year. William saw me getting bullied, decided to step in, and we had been friends since that day. I met Benjamin through William, and all three of us started to hang out together.

The air was fresh, and the sky was clear. We walked around playing on the block and decided to go to the convenience store we frequently visited. This store had one way in and one way out, and it was easy to dip and move behind things to avoid being seen while trying to steal. One of us would distract the store clerk while the other two stacked up on candy and whatever else we could fit in our pockets or inside the belt loops of our pants. Like always, we got away with it.

We ate our snacks and laughed as we walked back to Williams's house. We walked toward a group of kids. Some were our age, and a few were a little older. As we passed the older boys, they saw us eating the candy. One of them jumped up and told us to give it to him. Being the tougher one in our group, William instantly jumped in the front and said, "Hell no, get your own."

Before he could get the words out of his mouth, the older kid had punched him in the face. Williams's lip was split open, and his nose was bleeding. He started swinging back, and we all started fighting. We didn't stand a chance; too many of them were bigger and older than we were.

They beat us pretty badly and took all the snacks we had. Benjamin and I laughed about it after. It wasn't like we hadn't been in fights before. However, this was different for William because he felt he got the worst of it. The fact that an older kid had gotten the best of him made him angry because he was known to be a kid that could always hold his own.

He was built like Hulk and already had a reputation for being tough. We all soaked our wounds back at William's house while sitting outside. Benjamin and I tried to cheer William up and told him it wasn't a big deal. We told him the kid was much bigger and older, and he sucker-punched him. William was still mad and could only think about making them pay for what they had done to him. We didn't know what was going on or what was going through William's mind. Soon, William's older brother got home and was also a tough man. He was always fighting; he fought more than anyone I could remember at that age.

Once William's brother got home and saw his brother's lip busted, he was instantly furious. Several of his brother's friends came over within a few minutes, and they were all mad. We could hear them talking about making them pay. They were outraged because William told them it was an older kid. We knew it would be a lot of trouble, Williams's brother was well known, and he didn't play. I'm not sure if the kids who beat us up knew who William or his brother was, but I felt they were about to find out.

While we were standing outside, a car pulled up. William's brother goes over and talks to the driver of the car. He tells William, Benjamin, and I to get in the car to show him where the kids who fought us were. We did as he said, got in the car, and directed them to where the kids were. They drove by, and the kids were still standing outside; a few more had joined the group. It quickly went from day to night, and we were still driving around in the car. Passing the same area over and over to ensure they had not left. We thought William's brother and friends would soon get out and beat them all up. They drove past them once again, stopping about a half-block away. They turned the car around and parked on the side of the street.

The driver got out, opened the truck, and returned to the car with a bag. As he opened it, we saw it was a bag full of guns. William's brother and the driver started passing the guns around like snacks. William's brother got one, and the driver got one. Benjamin and I in the backseat are looking at each other with concern. However, William seemed to be all for what was happening. As we're sitting in the backseat, his brother turns to us and says, "Are y'all gonna handle y'all business or what?"

William is the first one to answer, "Hell yeah!" Benjamin and I sit there silently and shake our heads to affirm yes. We were fearful of what was about to happen. The driver looks at us and then hands us each a gun.

All three of us have guns in our hands now, and William's brother looks back and says, "Y'all gotta handle your business. If somebody pushes up on y'all, then y'all better learn how to push back. If not, they're gonna always be pushin' you." It made sense, but downright shooting them was more than I thought we should do. William's brother said, "When we drive up, hold your hands out of the window, and when I say shoot, then shoot. But wait for me to say it."

I'm looking at Benjamin and thinking, what are we doing, are we supposed to shoot them for taking our candy? This retaliation was more than I had planned. The whole situation is going way too far in my mind. William's brother must have read my mind and the look on my face. He looked at me and snarled, "They punched my little brother in the mouth and busted his lip. They have to pay." With that, we had no choice but to go along with it.

As we drove up the street, I had no clue if I would be able to pull the trigger. Williams's brother was reading my face again because just then, William's brother looked back at Benjamin and me to yell, "You motherfuckers better not be scared. When we drive by, you better start shooting. If you don't do what you are supposed to do, we will deal with you." My hands were shaking, and the gun felt heavy.

As we drive up next to the group of kids, everything starts to move in slow motion. William's brother whispered, "Get they asses," that was the quietest he had spoken the whole night. Although terrified, we did as we were told. I held my gun out the window, William and Benjamin right there by my side. Benjamin could not do it, and he dropped back into the seat as William let off the first shot while hanging out the window like a movie. Where did he learn this from, I was thinking. I shoot once and then a second time. The driver hit the gas hard, making me fall back into the seat.

With that quick motion, my third shot went into the roof of the car. We were driving fast, and it wasn't my fault the driver pulled off so quickly. Glass was all over the place, and we did not know where it came from. My immediate thought was that someone had thrown a bottle at the car. But that wasn't what it was. The driver had gotten shot in the arm and was cursing with blood everywhere, but he kept driving, and we could not believe what had just happened. I thought I was dreaming because of how well he had taken being shot. We were all freaking out, and William's brother told us to shut up. He dropped us off and told us to get out of the car, go inside and take showers.

We could not believe what had just happened. I was almost scared to even talk about it. I remember I could not sleep for a long time after that. I had countless nights of sweating and worrying, making me tired in school all day. I was terrified that someone was going to come and find me. That they would know who it was, and I would die. I had nightmares for weeks.

I was afraid to walk to and from school and terrified while in my house and school. That may have been the scariest time frame of my life. All I could think of was, what have I done? Had we hit anybody? A bunch of kids with guns never make a good combination, and something will always go wrong. Benjamin and I would not talk about this for days, even weeks. We had grown further away from William. We were unsure if we wanted to be around him because we didn't want his brother to make us go anywhere and do anything like that again. I learned a lot from that experience: never get in a car with older people.

CHAPTER 13 | MRS. COLEMAN

I think my third-grade teacher, Mrs. Coleman, knew something terrible had happened, or at least she could sense that I wasn't right. I think she knew I wasn't sleeping at night, and often she would be a little easier on me in class. She would always say extra nice things, telling me how great I could be if I only focused on being great. She told me she could see me being rich when I got older. I don't know how she could see that. I couldn't even see myself getting older, yet she could see me being rich and older. All the students used to think she was beautiful. We all thought she was the mother of NBA basketball player Derrick Coleman. That made me like her even more.

Mrs. Coleman understood me when I came to her class. She would always give me a high-five or a hug and ask me how my day was. I often focused on the negative, but she would stop me and ask me to tell her about the good parts of my day. I would focus on my day's positive and good aspects in those moments.

Third grade was a year of self-inflicted wounds and trauma-stricken decisions, mainly on behalf of my poor choices. I felt powerless and just wanted to live like a normal kid. But I always thought that I needed to live as an adult. Was I a precocious kid? Possibly at times, I was.

At this time, my brothers and I had finally made it over to Arizona street to live with my grandmother, Lil Freddie. Although there were still rough times because we often went without water and power. The environment was good because we were not living out of motels and random houses. It was by far better living with my grandmother Lil Freddie and Isaiah.

I was a child in many ways, but I felt I was far advanced in providing, protecting, and understanding what a man was supposed to be. I was a little boy who battled mentally with wanting to be a kid but needing to be a man. Emotionally I was at war with who I was as a child and how I was supposed to be an adult to survive. I was going to be rich, and not necessarily in a financial way but in the course of righteousness. I wanted to be better than everyone ever expected me to be. I had already been deemed a failure by most. I was the little, black, dirty kid who smelled terrible and was destined to be a failure. I could not read or spell and spent my time in Special Ed, so I was labelled as ignorant.

Sometimes when you do not have anyone to speak life to you, you have to find out how to do it yourself. You have to do things that bring meaning to your life. For me, that was helping others and protecting my siblings.

We all have instances in our lives that leave lasting impacts, times that demonstrate kindness and compassion for others. Mrs. Coleman was a teacher who was strict but loving. She would never take any crap from all of us 'bad' kids. She never judged us for what we did not know. She only wanted to measure what we did know and see improvement as the final result. She cared about our academic knowledge but also our self-awareness. She cared about what we thought of ourselves and how we conducted ourselves. She showed she cared and would find a way to relate to every kid, even when we were wrong.

Sometime during the third grade school year, we were getting ready to take a spelling test. It is safe to say I did not study not one bit, so I never even attempted to pass that test. But the day had come. Mrs. Coleman told us to put everything away and take out a sheet of paper and a pencil.

She began reading all ten spelling words one at a time while all the students successfully wrote them down. It would seem, with much ease and almost happiness, as I panned the room. I was angry; no one else seemed to be struggling as I was.

I was mad that I could not experience that same sense of assurance and joy. All I could think was what that felt like and where that confidence came from? I was cursing all those 'smart kids.' I wanted them to relinquish some of that confidence just so that I could feel it for once. I wanted to have that pride and joyous look. You know that look you have when you love someone or something. It was the look I wanted to have when I saw my finished test. I wanted to feel pride and joy when I turned it into Mrs. Coleman. But I knew that was not going to happen. My look was one of defeat, sadness, and embarrassment. The test was over, and everyone stood up to turn in their sheets of paper.

I was hanging at the back of the class to go last. I did not want anyone to see these words, or maybe I should not even call them words. It was a list of letters, set together in the order of chaos. For example, awesome might look like 'osome' or school would look like 'scool.' There would be some words that I did know, but when I tried to write them, the letters would jump around. Therefore, I would put them out of order even if I did know how to spell them. I stopped trying to figure out why those things happened long ago and figured out how to fix them.

The day after the spelling test Mrs. Coleman called me up to the front of the class and asked me if I had studied for the test, and of course, I lied and said yes. She told me I had missed them all and got a zero on the test. I was devastated because although I knew the words were hard to spell and most likely I did not know many of them, I was hoping to at least get one of them right.

Instantaneously, I felt dumb and unworthy. My head went down, and my shoulders sank in. Mrs. Coleman quickly told me not to do that; you are better than this. She kindly said to me that my greatness was only up to me. I was so shocked and had never heard anything like that before.

Up to that point, I don't remember ever having a teacher tell me anything positive like that. She explained that she could tell I did not study for the test, and the only way I would have a chance to pass these tests was to practice like all the other kids. At that age, I had no idea what it was to study. She allowed me to retake the test if I promised to study the words. I did my best and studied for about two days, and then it was time to retake the test. I knew I was not going to be ready for this test. I was preparing to be even more embarrassed and humiliated than I was the first time. So, I got together with my inner self and developed a plan to get a 100% on the test.

The night before, I pulled out all the words and looked at them. I started to study for a few minutes before I had an external interruption in the form of my mother telling me that I had to come and clean the kitchen. So there goes my study plan. Because I could not tell my mom, I was busy studying and asking her to get someone else to do the job. That would have been followed immediately by 'what did you say?' Like most black communities of that time, there was no speaking your mind or feelings in our house.

We never had a dialogue between the family about our feelings and needs. You just did what was asked of you or got a beating. That was just the way it was. After cleaning the kitchen, I had to get my brothers ready for bed and get their clothes ready for school. Mom then told me to go to bed myself. Once again, I could not say, hey, mom, I have to study for a spelling test before bed. It just didn't happen that way.

I woke up the next morning scared of what would happen on this test. I got the bright idea of writing all the words down and turning that sheet in as the finished test. Then I wrote all the words from the book in order. I put the paper in my folder and headed to school with my head held high because I knew this would be my first 100% on a test. I met with Mrs. Coleman, sat down, and numbered my paper. She starts with word number one, then two, until she finishes all ten words. I am just writing random letters as she says the words because I know I have all the correct spellings in my folder.

Now the test is over, and it is time to make the switch. How will I pull this one-off? I had to be super careful, mainly because we were the only ones in the classroom. She heads back to her desk, and that is when I thought to myself, do it! Paper out, other paper in, and I had gotten away with the best move of the year! No more zero for me on a spelling test! I had the key; I knew how to pull it off now. Later that day, Mrs. Coleman pulled me to the side to congratulate me on getting a 100% on the test. I was so excited and understood the other kids' pride. Even if it were fake manufactured happiness, I would sell myself on this lie because it felt great. Soon the next test was approaching, but I was not worried. I had prepared my sheet the same way, and Mrs. Coleman started to read off the words.

Again, I am confident I will do well because I have the secret! The test was over, and I made an easy switch. I dance to the front of the room, graceful and proud. I handed my paper to Mrs. Coleman, then turned and walked back to my desk, but my return walk was all confident swag this time. It felt like a great day.

The next day Mrs. Coleman is handing out the graded test with a smile from ear to ear. I can see the proud mom look in her eyes; she was so happy for the students because they had all done so well. I could not wait until she got over to me to give me that look as she reached my desk, her face dropped, with no smile and no happy eyes. She gets right in front of me and says, "I am very disappointed in you." Then she sat my test on the desk, and there were red checks on all ten words. I was confused and did not understand why I had gotten a zero instead of the 100% I knew I should have gotten. The 100% that I lied to myself about deserving. Mrs. Coleman finished passing out the other papers, and she called me up to her desk. I asked her why I had gotten a zero; she calmly said, "Because you cheated."

"No, I did not," I managed to get out with a straight face. She called another student and asked for him to bring her his test. This student always got 100's, so I could not wait to show her that all the words would be spelt just like his list. This kid handed her his paper, and she sat it next to mine. "What is the first word on his paper?" she asked. I could not even say the word. "Is it the same word as your number one?" I felt confused and stunned. It was not the same word. She then asked me, "Is his word listed by number two the same as yours?" It was not, and then I started to catch on.

Mrs. Coleman was an intelligent woman. She'd known what I did the previous week but did not call me out for it. She could not prove it, so she did something better. She gave the test out of order and caught me cold. I could not explain myself away from how this had happened. I was busted, and I had to accept that.

That day Mrs. Coleman spoke some of the most powerful words I had ever heard. She said, "You are a much brighter kid than you give yourself credit for. Yes, it is wrong that you cheated, but you were in a situation where you had to find a way out, and you did. It didn't work, but you tried. That means something, and you should just remember to put that same energy into finding a way to do things right. Use that energy to study or ask for help." This lesson taught me a lot about life. Cutting corners, while easier in the moment, never helped anyone achieve greatness.

It's funny how the strictest teacher, the hardest one on you, sometimes turns out to be your favorite. I remember telling Mrs. Coleman that I wanted to be righteous, and she said being righteous started with being an honest man. She told me I had to have integrity first. I had no clue what that word meant at the time. But as I grew up, I came to understand and search for just that. After that encounter, I tried to discover and seek integrity and righteousness.

I had no idea that her words would mean so much to me and stay with me as they have. But they did, and I can only hope that there are many more Mrs. Colemans for children today that need someone like her.

She made me think about the way I wanted to treat people. She made me care about education when I hated everything about learning. She made me believe in myself when I thought negatively of myself every day. She forced smiles on my face when I only wanted to be angry. When I didn't have food, she would give me her lunch. She showed that she cared, not just pretending to care but genuinely caring, and I think some people get confused about those differences. Some people never realize that caring is not always being soft; sometimes, it is having hard conversations. But true tough love teaches valuable lessons.

As a young black inner-city kid who was poor and lacked discipline, constantly abused, beaten up, and mistreated, I needed Mrs. Coleman. She instilled discipline, righteousness, ethical values, and morals within me. She applied affirmations that I had never heard, reassuring me that I was good even when I didn't believe it. She assured me that if I listened, paid attention, and gave my all, I could be anything and everything I wanted. She was right!

CHAPTER 14 | FIRST JOB

At ten years old, I was still small for my age and dirty. Most days, I walked around with dirty clothes, shoes with soles ripped open, and socks that you could smell through my shoes. I usually wore too small, highwater pants and some oversized hand-me-down shirts. I was in third grade, and the year had been a strange one so far.

I was still living in Joliet, Illinois, with my grandma and grandpa at this time. One of the many stints we had over there. It would often happen when my mom was in an in-between situation. That could mean with her boyfriend, my dad, or any other reason that would drive us back to being with my grandparents and a better living situation.

Thinking about it now, it's funny what I considered good living back then. We often would not have running water or electricity, yet living there was by far the most luxurious option we had. I remember stealing electricity from the next-door neighbors and going to the well to fill a bunch of jugs of water so that we would have water in the house to bathe, cook and flush the toilet at times. I would always have to share bath water with my brothers.

My uncle would also live there with us; he was so cool and clean. He was tall and always dressed nicely. I looked up to him because he was older than us but not too old that he could not understand what we were going through. Most of the time, I wanted to be like the adults I had seen on TV. But I also had men in my life that I was inspired to be like.

My grandfather Isaiah was one of those men. I wanted to work hard and take care of my family, get a paycheck and take my kids out to do something fun, just like my grandfather did for me. Isaiah Johnson was his name, he was not my biological grandfather, but he had been in my life since I was small. This man did more for me than any other man in my life. He was a substantial role model and was always there to pull my grandma, Lil Freddie, off my back when I continued to get in trouble. He was consistent and showed me what it looked like to take care of your family and provide everything needed to survive. He did not have a lot, but he ensured we would always get a piece of what he did.

I had that urge to provide at an early age. So, I always tried to make extra money to feed myself and have a little extra cash. Sometimes five or ten dollars a week was all I was trying to get. I would feel like a rich man if I could do twenty dollars in a week. In the early 1990s, twenty dollars a week for a 10-year-old was astonishing. I felt like I had hit the big time. I used to walk around the neighborhood looking for things to do and different ways to make money.

I stopped at a store named Washington Square. Washington Square sat on the corner of a street with a small parking lot. Across the street from this store sat a little house. A classmate of mine we called white boy Tom lived there with his family. Tom was not well-liked at school; everyone picked on him because he had a big mouth. He was always tattling on people, and he was the teacher's little snitch.

I walked into Washington Square and told the manager that the garbage was full and spilling out. He told me to get out unless I was going to buy something. As I walked out, I said, okay, but there's still trash all over the place. I stood outside for an hour thinking about what I could do to make some money. I came up with the idea to show the store owner he needed me and that I could be of good use. I started taking the trash out of the garbage can and throwing it all over the parking lot. Once I finished, I went back inside and told him to come to look at all the trash on his lot. The wind is blowing it all over the place. The store owner came outside and started cursing and yelling as the garbage was blown around by the strong gust of wind that had magically appeared at the perfect moment.

Since the store owner was standing outside, I decided to take full advantage of the situation. I ran around, grabbed as much trash as possible, and returned it to the garbage can. Eventually, I asked if he had another bag. The owner went back inside to grab more sacks. Once he went inside, I pushed the whole trash can over to make an even bigger mess. He came back, and I began picking the trash up to show how much work needed to be done. He saw my hard work and asked if I would stay longer and pick it up. I said yes and asked how much he would pay me. He said ten dollars, and I almost fell over thinking about that amount of money and what I could do with it. I finished picking up all the trash I had helped disperse and went inside to tell him I was done. He paid me and told me to stop by a few times a week to clean and take out the trash, and just like that, I officially had a job.

Working there was amazing, and having my own money was great. Even though I was only in third grade, I felt a sense of independence. I felt rich with ten dollars a week when things rarely cost over twenty-five cents. Back then, you could even get the real penny candy. That would be one-hundred pieces of candy for one dollar, and that's a lot of candy!

I was so happy I could not wait to get to school and tell my teacher Mrs. Coleman about my real job. I knew she would be proud of me because she would always tell me how great I could be if I just put my mind to it. I worked at the store for a few months, getting my ten dollars weekly.

I woke one Saturday morning to a deafening silence. I was usually overwhelmed by sounds I usually could not hear. Living in the hood was weird like that. I listened to my heartbeats while thinking of my plans for the day. What would I eat, what would I wear? What type of trouble would I get in? Will I get yelled at or do something that requires a beating? I was thinking about the trouble I might get into for waking up too early. I knew my bladder was screaming for help and a bathroom, but I was scared to get up and make too much noise in the silence. I believe most people don't understand these types of thoughts the little black boy has to contemplate.

I finally started my day; I went to the refrigerator, looked for something to eat, and came up short. There was some food, but only things that needed to be cooked, nothing fast like cereal or a pop tart. I decided to put clothes on to go outside to freedom. Somewhere we could go to have fun and be free to smile and think positively. Once I was out, I met up with some friends, and we quickly came up with the idea to go to the store to get the food we wanted for breakfast. We sat off to Washington Square, and as we were walking around the corner, my brother Taiwan came running up to us and wanted to go. So, we let him. We took a shortcut through an ally surrounded by garbage cans and an old mattress we would do backflips on.

Whenever you landed on one of these mattresses, you would get a fresh burst of pee-scented air. But we did not care; we were free to have fun and run and play as we wanted. Once we reached the store, we saw other kids throwing rocks at the cars driving by. We hid on the side of the store and joined in throwing rocks at the passing cars. I know it was crazy; we would hit the windows, and the vehicles would slam on their brakes, so we would take off running and hide. It seemed like so much fun, but I know it was stupid thinking about it now. We could have hurt someone.

I do not know where it came from, but soon someone showed up with a crowbar. We started playing with the crowbar, then suddenly it was in my hands, and I was using it to pop the lock on the store door. I don't remember what I was thinking then, and I don't know how the door opened, but it did. We glanced at each other with sheer amazement on our faces. We were dumbfounded because we didn't know what to do. We had the opportunity to have snacks and everything else in the store that we could carry. But this is where I was working, and I knew it was a dumb idea. But again, I overlooked the voice that told me not to do it. There was no one there to tell us that we couldn't have it, so that's what we did. We took all that we could carry and had no idea what to do with it, but we did not seem to care. We were poor kids running the streets with nothing to eat. What would people expect to happen in that situation?

After grabbing as much food as we wanted, we started jumping on the counters and took Bulls short sets. They had red, white, black, and different color pinstripes. The Bulls were very popular in the '90s. In 1991-1993 when the Bulls were at their best, Michael Jordan was the world's greatest basketball player. These short sets were something everybody wanted. So, we took as many as we could carry and just ran them back around the corner to our house, and then we would come back for more.

My uncle was at home at the time. He was only 20 years old, but he was grown. He saw us when we returned to the house and asked where we got all this stuff. We could not lie and say someone gave it to us or we had found it; he would know better. He also knew we didn't have enough money to buy it. So, we had to tell the truth. I told him we got it from the store, but he asked how. I tried to say somebody had just left the door open, so he asked if we had stolen it all. I hesitated for a second because I did not want to get in trouble, and then my friend's big mouth blurted out, "Yeah, we took all of it, and there's a lot more left." My uncle Edward looked right at me with a look of shock. I knew he was about to slap the crap out of me and tell me how crazy it was for me to take it all. But to my surprise, he did not do that. His response was, "For real? Go get some more!"

So that's what we did. We ran back around the corner and into the store and grabbed as much more as we could carry. We came out of the store laughing, but there was a problem. We looked across the street this time, and white boy Tom was staring at us. Tom knew who I was, so we took off running. We got back to my house, and I told my uncle that the white boy Tom had seen us. He knew who I was and that he would probably tell someone. My uncle said, "Fuck him, and if he tells you, better beat his ass."

We all eyed each other with a look of understanding. A few minutes had passed, and we were trying on the clothes, thinking we were looking fly. But the shorts hung down to our ankles, and the shirts were way too long for us. We look more like a '90s boy band than a bunch of cool hip kids. But we did not care, we were still clean, and we had a bunch of snacks to eat.

Spirits were high but was the excitement about to end? I could not help but wonder if Tom knew who it was in the store. Would the police be on our block soon? Whatever maybe I was overthinking it. I should have just been thinking about enjoying myself. But like always, I think past the moment and start wondering about the what if's.

CHAPTER 15 | FIRST ARREST

Like many moments in my life, I would find out that being a bad person was not in the cards for me. It seemed like every time I did something wrong, the universe would fight with me to get back on the right track. That track would always involve punishment and a lesson that I was supposed to get from my actions. Breaking into Washington Square would be no different.

During our celebration, the police had made their way to our block. I was left wondering if it was just their routine or were they looking for someone. They did not know who had broken into the store, but since we were all standing in front of the house and matched the police description of a group of 'young black boys,' we stuck out like a sore thumb. In fairness, they had been right in this instance, but often they are not. I have been on both ends of this type of situation.

After riding up and down the streets a few times, they finally stopped at my house, and everyone took off running. I had no choice but to stay because it was our house, and I thought I knew what I was doing. I had watched enough TV to know they couldn't just come into our house without a warrant. Yes, I knew this at the age of ten.

They asked me what my name was and where I went to school. Like the smartass I thought I was, I told them I did not have to talk to them without a lawyer. The police told my uncle that somebody had told them we were in the store. They knew it was us, so they arrested me.

The police officer was friendly, he told me I was getting ready to go with him, and my uncle could come. I was scared, and I had no idea what to do. My uncle told me to shut up and not say anything. I didn't listen; I asked the police all types of questions. Where are we going? What did I do? When am I coming back? The police officer said to relax, and once we got to the station, he was sure my family would come and get me. He had no idea who my family was, as if he thought they would be down anytime soon to pick me up. We got to the police station, and they put me in a room alone, where I would sit for at least an hour before anyone came to talk to me. The police officer who brought me down came in and gave me a pop to drink.

I was thankful because he was treating me well. The officer told me how much trouble I was in. I think he just wanted me to tell the truth. He talked calmly and explained that he did not want to see me get in trouble. I crossed my arms and sat back in the cold chair. I look at the police officer with one of those 'I don't give a shit' looks. I gave my shoulders a giant shrug like I was some rich white kid with a father to bail them out of anything. But after a few seconds of holding my cool, that look turned into genuine fear because I knew I had no one like that.

I had been sitting in that room for a long time, hoping my uncle would come and get me, but he never came. The police officer returned to the room and asked me again if I understood how much trouble I was in. He then said someone across the street had seen me and some other boys running out of the store. White boy Tom strikes again, and I should have known. It was the first time I realized the severity of what I had done. I kept thinking, why am I so dumb? I can't even read and am just the stupid, dirty, little black boy. This thought would pop into my mind many times throughout my childhood. Because I heard it so much, I started to believe it. It was one thing when my classmates would say the words, but who was I not to believe it when adults, family members, and even teachers would say it? The police officer put a piece of paper on the table in front of me. "These are the rights that you have when you get arrested. Go ahead and read them."

The fear was back, but it was not because I feared going to jail. The fear stemmed from the certain embarrassment I was about to face for not knowing a single word on this paper. At this time, I could not read very well, if at all. I stared hard at the paper, thinking words would read themselves. I looked at each sentence on the page, hoping to recognize at least one or two. Unfortunately, I could not read one word. I had no clue what was on this paper. The officer said to go ahead and read it, so I yelled, "I don't have to read this shit."

Like many times in school, I chose angry deflection when called on to read or answer a question. Instead of letting people know I could not read, I would lash out and start cursing or hitting someone. Sometimes, I would even get up and flip my desk to get kicked out of class so I did not have to read out loud or answer a question. But with that behavior, I was always labelled as just a bad kid.

The officer again asked me to read it, and I looked at him, grabbed the paper, and balled it up. I will never forget this exchange that occurred next. He said, "Your little black ass can't read, can you?" He laughed as he walked out of the room. When he came back, he had two other officers with him. One had another sheet of paper in her hand. The first officer said, "Go ahead, give it to his black ass." I had heard that language towards me so much that it didn't bother me, even if it came from a white person. So, she sat the sheet of paper down, and the first officer again told me to read it.

I was thinking, why would he ask me to read again? He knows I can't read this. So, I stared at the page as if I was reading it. The first officer kicked my chair and said, "Read it out loud, muthafucker." I looked up at him with disappointment and sadness because I thought he was one of the good ones. But then he started laughing again and said, "His black ass can't even read one word." I was devastated after that. I felt stupid and even believed that no one could ever protect me; if I could not trust the police to protect me, then who would.

At that point, I retreated into my thoughts and took myself back to that old and scary basement that my foster mother used to lock me in. I found that space as I sat and hoped someone would come to get me. Would anyone even come, or would I possibly be sent back to a foster home or juvenile detention? The fear tried to sneak in, but as I learned so many other times, it was ultimately up to me to fight it and not allow it in. I told myself whatever I had to fight it, that I did not care if I had to go back to a foster home. I am ready for anything.

CHAPTER 16 | RESCUED AGAIN

Time after time, there has always been one man in my life that has always been there for me. One who would defend me even when I was wrong. And on this day that I thought no one would come to get me from the police station, he showed up for me again. After a few hours, my grandfather Isaiah showed up to bring me home. Isaiah met my grandmother a few years after I was born.

Ultimately, I had not gotten into much trouble with the police from breaking into the store. I assume it was because there were a lot of kids involved from the neighborhood, and they could not pin it on one person, but no one ever told me why.

But it was not the trouble with the police that I was upset over. It was the look that my grandfather Isaiah was giving me that hurt my heart. He was disappointed in me because he wanted me to be a better person. I was more crushed that I had upset and disappointed him than I was about being taken to the police station. Grandpa Isaiah was the type of old-school man I loved and looked up to, so I had wished he was around me every day. He was compassionate, patient, and understanding.

Grandpa Isaiah would sit me down and talk to me about how a man should act and how he was supposed to treat his wife. He also taught me how to forgive kids for making mistakes. He was a great man who taught me so much. If I could have been around him more, I would have been much better off.

One day we were laughing with my grandmother Lil Freddie. She asked Isaiah what he would do if she found a new man. He laughed and said, "Nothing, I'd just have to go." She asked if she would be able to keep the house. He said, "Yep," and turned to me, "It doesn't matter what happens. As a man, you never take anything from your family. If it doesn't work out, you let your family have everything and find out how to make it all back." Those were the lessons that Isaiah would always try to give me.

After leaving the police department, I received a stern talking to filled with that old-school tough love, designed only to help me see that I could do better. I hoped that one day I could be the man he thought I could be.

When I think about how much I wanted to be like him as a kid, I remember my grandma, Lil Freddie, saying, "He is only this good of a man because I taught him." I often laugh thinking about that statement because I know that my grandma was such a good-hearted woman that I believe she did teach him. My grandfather was not the only positive force in my life as I started to get older. There was also the feisty influence of my grandmother, who would constantly try to will the greatness out of me.

I
s
a
i

ah and I

Smooth dressing Grandfather Isaiah

CHAPTER 17 | MY ANGEL

Besides the time when my grandma sent me back to that motel, she had been the most consistent and loving person in my life for as long as I could remember. She was my constant sunshine whenever we were lucky enough to be around her. I know my dad and mom did love me. There were just no actions that I can recall that showed it. I remember often laughing with my grandma. She would take us shopping to buy school clothes and food from White Castle or Brown's Chicken. My grandma would cook us meals, give us treats and talk to us about what was right and wrong.

My grandparents were like our second set of parents. But they were older, more mature, and prepared. Their lives had calmed down, and as we all understand, when that happens in life, older parents tend to go easier on the kids. My grandparents, Lil Freddie and Isaiah, did all their partying and had all their wild times at a young age. My grandma was working and understood a little better how to take care of children. We learned lessons, observed actions, and saw positive reinforcement and loving actions daily when living with them.

One day I got home from school, and my socks and shoes were soaking wet because of all the snow I had to walk in to get home. I took the long route because it was the start of Christmas break, and I was afraid to go home.

I know what everyone is thinking. Why would you be scared to go home on Christmas break? Well, the last day of school for the fall semester also meant report card time. In my book bag would be a report card that would not be very favorable to my behind. I was surely going to get a whooping if I took these grades home.

So, I devised a great plan as I took the long route home. I took the report card out and decided to alter the grades to slightly better ones. I got home and gave my grandmother, Lil Freddie, my report card. She gazed over at me with the biggest smile on her face, reached for me, and gave me the biggest hug, followed by excitement and kind words.

She called my siblings into the living room along with my grandfather, Isaiah. I was on cloud nine because I had pulled off the biggest hoax of Christmas break. She passed the report card to Isaiah first; after careful examination, he gave me some great words of love and excitement. I was all smiles, so I took the report card from my grandfather and showed it to my sister Tasha. Tasha was the oldest, and she was intelligent and hard to fool.

Tasha took one look at my report card and started laughing. I asked what she was laughing at, and she said that I didn't really get all B's. I yelled at her, calling her names and getting mad. This time, she repeated it even louder that these were not all B's. She told me that I had changed all the F's to B's, and then I got mad because she was correct in her accusation. I had altered the report card full of F's to B's and had successfully tricked my grandparents.

As Tasha and I argued, my grandmother asked to see the report card again and quickly agreed with my sister. She asked if I had changed the grades, and at that point, I had to be honest. I told her yes, I had changed the grades. I knew I was about to be in big trouble.

My grandma stood up and told me to follow her. We walked into the living room and sat on the couch. She asked why I had changed the grades, and I explained that I was scared to make her mad at me, and I did not want her to know that I was not smart. She paused and looked at me in my eyes, and I could feel the pain she had on her face.

The hurt on her face was because of the negative outlook of my self-worth. She did not say anything right away; she just hugged me. She then told me not ever to say anything like that again. She said I just needed to try hard and do what I was supposed to do in school and that I could do anything I set my mind to. After that pep talk, she played some old-school music while we sat on the couch talking for about an hour about my dreams and what I wanted to do when I got older.

Grandma was a few years older than my grandpa, and they met while working at a nursing home. She already had children from her previous relationships, and he took them all in and loved them as his own. I've always looked up to him because he was the first figure in my life that attempted to teach me how to be a man and show me how to treat a spouse. I'll never forget the lessons he taught me about life and always be thankful for him. He took on this relationship with a woman who already had five kids with multiple fathers. He loved her for who she was, and he loved all her kids just like they were his own. He spent more time with her children and grandchildren than with his own family. I'm sure that caused problems in his past relationships with his children; how could it not?

Although my grandma had his support and worked an excellent job to provide, it wasn't easy when she had us all there. But neither of them would ever let us know they were struggling to provide. I remember when we had no running water for months and no electricity for weeks. During those times without it, we could run an extension cord out our window through the bushes, plug it in the house next door, and steal electricity until we got ours turned back on.

My grandma was like superwoman to me; she was tough and always had our backs. Many times she sent me outside to get a rematch of a fight that I had lost. I learned most of my cooking skills from my grandmother.

Despite all the hardships, we had food, a home to live in, and, most importantly, love within the household. My grandma watched me play high school football and often showed up to my wrestling matches. My granny and I would also often have conversations about the woman I was dating in my life, and she would give me the best advice and always preach being respectful.

Because my grandma was that remarkable woman in my life, I always saw it as having two moms. She raised me most of the time, and when I was young, it was hard to understand how to separate the two. For the longest time, she was the most loving and consistent person in my life; I am eternally grateful for that.

Lil Freddie being sexy
Willamae

Lil Freddie and Step-Grandma

Lil Freddie and husband Isaiah

My Grandmother Lil Freddie

142

CHAPTER 18 | BIG BLUE

This was a challenging year for me, I was still ten years old, and it seemed I could not catch a break from turmoil. Although I was still living with my grandparents, and they were doing their best to promote good morals in me, I was still having a hard time accepting that I could be better than what I was when I was outside of my home. It was easy to migrate to situations that would cause problems in my life.

I was still dealing with the effects of not having much in the way of material things and not being very smart. I was not reading well and was still doing poorly in school. I had no foundation on how to study or do school work, so I found being in the school building very stressful and challenging to deal with. I was severely bullied every day, so I started skipping school and breaking into multiple homes. I found it to be easier to abandon the situation altogether.

I had good people that would try to speak life into me, but I could not hear them over the sounds of hunger from my belly. Or from the sounds of constant teasing for being poor, dirty, or dumb. I could not block out the noise blasting so loud from others. Nonetheless, a few friends of mine would meet up every morning. We would collect enough cans or steal enough materials and scrap metal to turn into the junkyard for a few dollars. After collecting our money, we would scramble to the nearest gas station.

There we could buy a few hundred pieces of penny candy. We had been establishing this tradition for the past few weeks. More and more kids started to join us, but we had created something that was getting too big to control. Kids were ditching every other day and going around to collect materials before we could get to them. It started making us mad because it was cutting into our candy money.

Once we bought our candy, we would take it to this truck junkyard. It had empty semi-truck trailers, which is where we would hang out. One blue truck trailer made for an excellent clubhouse. We stole a few blankets to keep in there to sleep sometimes. The first time we found it, we cleaned it like our new home. There was wood and nails all over the place. I swept the area well and found some boxes we used for dressers or nightstands. We even put posters on the walls.

On the days I was in school, I would see some kids rushing to get home to their parents and family. But not me. I wanted to do everything in my power to keep from going home. This getaway clubhouse made us the men of our own place. We kept it clean, and we could let in or keep out anyone we wanted. We controlled the environment and everything that came with it. We tried to keep this place positive and fun.

We used this clubhouse for about two weeks, and no one bothered us. One morning we woke up just like we had the last few weeks. We met outside near the brick house on the corner. I arrived first and waited several minutes for my friend Tim. As I was standing outside, a policeman drove by, and I thought he would say something since we should have been in school. But he only glanced at me and continued to drive past. I was nervous at such a close call and wished Tim would hurry. Standing there had made me hungry because I could smell hickory-smoked bacon and eggs being cooked nearby. I snapped out of this food fantasy as Tim came running up, carrying two black plastic bags bigger than usual.

We started walking up the street, but I told him we better move through some of the allies because of the cop that had driven by earlier. He laughed it off and stated we were faster than them anyway. We continued walking around with plastic bags in hand, collecting our cans and other things we could take to the scrap yard. It was a straightforward way to make some quick money. We had embraced that we would not make much money, but things did not cost a lot back then either. The only obstacle we faced was other collectors getting the stuff before us.

As the day went by, we found ourselves satisfied with the number of things we had collected, and it was time to go turn it in. We headed to the junkyard, and just like other days, there was a long line. We just stood there waiting our turn, laughing, and talking about how much money we thought we would get that day.

When it was finally our turn, we stepped up to the man who always took our stuff. I remember we were so afraid of him because he was a big man with a long grey beard. He had rough hands and a deep Barry White kind of voice. He was always mean but mean in a friendly way. He was mean, like a father figure. He would tell us what the best stuff was to bring and where we could find a lot of it. Every time we would step up to give him are stuff, he would say, "What the fuck do you little shits want today?"

I don't know why I always got a kick out of him talking to us like that. It did not bother me because the jab was always followed by something positive with his raspy laugh, "The harder you work, the better off you will be, damn it," or "Every other day I have to see y'all little shits, but at least you'll work hard." We would give him our stuff, and he would say, "Y'all, don't have anything worth anything." But he would always give us about five dollars apiece and say, "Now get away from me." We would say thank you, laugh, and run away. Strangely, it felt warm.

We headed right around the corner to the gas station, where we would always buy our stuff. We had been going so much lately that the gas station clerk started to trust us to count the penny candy ourselves.

Like most kids, my friend Tim would always want to add more to his mix. I wanted to also and used to do so until I watched some show that talked about the importance of doing the right thing when people were not watching you. After watching that show, I realized the importance of people trusting me. We got our candy and a pop of our choice to wash all the candy down. We quickly headed back to our clubhouse with our goods.

Unfortunately, this private clubhouse experience was soon coming to an end. Later that day, some other kids came down to the truck yard and played around. They came over to our clubhouse and saw how we had it set up, and they liked it. So, they picked their trailer and tried to set it up like ours. But after they finished, it did not look as good, so they were mad and hating on us.

We had already said we didn't want any negativity around our clubhouse, so we told them they could not stay around. They got angry, and one of them started throwing rocks at us, so we threw some back. One of the rocks hit my friend Tim, and he started crying.

Tim had been the only person who was nice to me and did not make fun of me, and he was like a brother to me. I felt I had to look after him, and I had to protect him. I had failed at this by letting him get hit with a rock, so I got angry and started to rage. I began to scream and started throwing anything I could get my hands on at those kids. I didn't care what it was. I ran toward the other kids, getting hit by the rocks they were throwing.

Without thinking, I grabbed a stone and a brick, not paying attention to how big the brick was. I pulled my arm back and threw that brick as hard as possible at one of the kids, hoping it hit one of them. Seconds after I had released the brick, we heard a blood-curdling scream.

Everything stopped; even Tim stopped crying and came over. The kid was lying on the ground bleeding all over and holding the side of his mangled face. No one wanted to touch him, and we had no idea what to do. Now I was scared, and I thought I would go to jail. Tim and I took off running.

We attempted to cross the street, but I was not paying enough attention because I got hit by a car. My body hit a police car hard, and I was shocked and scared. I remember feeling around to see if all my limbs were still attached.

The cop got out of the car, grabbed me off the ground, and threw me against it. The cop yelled at me, asking what I was doing in the streets. I looked over, and I could see Tim running and then stopping to watch what was happening from a safe distance. I told the cop I was on my way to school since I had gotten hit right in front of it.

I didn't even have a shirt on, so he knew I was lying. He rammed my head against the police car and told me not to be a smartass. He got into his car and pulled it right alongside the curb. He then walked back and put his hand around my neck as he snarled and pulled me to my feet. As I tried to move a little to get his hand off my neck, he tightened his grip. We began walking down the sidewalk towards the school, just a few yards down the street.

We stepped into the front office, and he made me give them my name. Still, with his hand gripped around the back of my neck as if I were going to try to run, he asked the secretary if I was a student there. She told him that I was one of their students and told him to release my neck. She responded calmly but firmly, "He is our student, so leave him here."

I am so thankful for this woman because I thought he would hurt me the way he talked. This interaction would have a lasting influence on how I felt about all police since then, the complete disappointment in a group of people supposed to protect me. This interaction was also one of the times that I can point to where my anger became determination. I was starting to transform into someone who could take care of myself by any means. Even though I was a fan of Malcolm X, I had not experienced or personally seen some of the injustices he and other black leaders would speak of so often. However, this opened my eyes to what I had heard about. This transformed my thoughts, and I would not realize how much until years later.

I walked away with only a busted lip, but it was the first clear memory I had of being blatantly mistreated by the police... I thought they were supposed to be good people, protectors. But I learned that many were protectors of only some people and that not all of them were good.

I mention this story because we know that so many children are convinced that what their parents say and feel is how they are supposed to feel. Many believe that they are supposed to be just like their parents. I was never taught to hate any person or the police. But I was taught about the many injustices many black people had been victims of. This was when I started to believe that maybe the police did have something against us. Later in life, I would learn a harsh lesson that would challenge my stance.

CHAPTER 19 | FIRE AND DESIRE

There is one incident that I think had a significant impact on how I perceived myself and life at the time. In the fourth grade, we were back with our mom and lived in this two-story yellow house right across the street from the elementary school.

The place was decent for us, but the kitchen was awful, and the downstairs toilet was broken. We kept a bucket in that bathroom filled with water to pour into the toilet and force it to flush after we had done our business. We made sure to use it and refill it for the next person to use each time. That bucket of water will be significant later on in this story.

Like most days, we were home alone. My brothers and I were upstairs watching TV but in different rooms. I don't remember what show I was watching, but something spectacular came across the screen. Someone had poured gasoline in a long line towards a car, they threw a small lighter onto the starting point, and the flame roared and chased itself until it reached the car and blew it up. I don't know why I was so fascinated by this. Maybe it was the speed at which the flames travelled to the car, but I desperately wanted to try it. I looked around the room for something long, and it would let me see the flame chase itself to the end. I found some old Christmas wrapping paper and thought that would be just right.

I started to unroll it from one wall to the other end of the room, but our bunk beds were in the way, so I couldn't roll it as far as I wanted to. But with a bright idea, I pushed it under the bunk bed until it hit the wall and thought it would be an awesome wall-to-wall light show. I suppose only a child who had to use a big imagination to entertain himself and his siblings would come up with this idea without the thought of dreadful consequences.

Nonetheless, I grabbed a lighter and lit the end of the paper, expecting the magic to happen. It started to burn, and I was getting excited, but it was slow, nothing like the lightning speed of the fire trail on TV. What had I done wrong? I thought to myself and was so caught up in the fact it was not going as fast as I wanted that I did not realize how big the fire was getting.

The paper was shrinking and burning up closer and closer to the bed until it finally reached and caught the sheet hanging off the bottom bunk. I broke from my hypnosis and realized how bad this was getting. I ran to pull the sheet off the bed, but it got stuck and hung directly above the flame. The whole sheet had caught fire by that point, and I started to panic. In a flash of a moment, I was scared of how out of hand the fire had become, trying to figure out what to do and terrified of what my mother would do to me when she got home. Then I remembered the bucket.

I ran down the stairs as fast as possible and tried to grab the bucket. Because we only ever used it to pour into the toilet, I did not realize how heavy it was—trying to maneuver up the steep stairs one at a time, having to sit it down and adjust my grip every few steps. All while water was sloshing out with every bump. As I reached the top, I saw smoke and noticed my brothers standing in the hallway with fear in their eyes, having no idea where the smoke was coming from. They asked me what happened, but all I could say was to get into their room away from the smoke. I should have told them to get outside right then, but I wasn't thinking clearly.

I continued down the hall and was confident I could get the fire out with this bucket. But when I stepped into the room, the flames were huge, and the tiny splash that I could get out after spilling most of the water on the stairs did nothing to damper the fire. I was terrified and out of ideas. I heard my brothers screaming behind me. I yelled at them to get outside, and we all ran down the stairs.

Once outside, we started to yell at the neighbors to help, but one had already called the fire department. My brothers and I were so scared and all yelling and crying. I don't know if we were crying because of the fire or the beating we knew would be coming from our mom. But then I looked around and realized my youngest brother was not there. I started running around frantically, looking through the yard to see if he had run off somewhere to hide. It was then I realized he was still inside. My whole body was numb with fear. Fear for my brother but also fear for myself.

As a child, I often feared being killed by my mom for my mistakes. But with that fear, I knew that I had to get my brother out of that house, I may die trying, but I would die for sure if I didn't get him out. I truly felt that way because I could not separate a regular beating from the feeling of someone trying to kill me. Was it as bad as I thought it was, or because I was a child, I thought it was worse?

By that time, a crowd had gathered, and I remember someone saying, "Their momma is gonna kill them." So that validated my thoughts at the time.

I ran towards the house, and someone else shouted, "What are you doing, boy?"

I just yelled back, "My brother is in there." I kept running, even though I heard him say to wait for the fire department. I could hear the sirens getting close, but I knew I had to save my brother, so I continued. I wanted to be the type of man who would do anything to protect his family, and I wanted to be the hero.

I stepped inside, and thankfully the fire had stayed confined to the upstairs. I spotted him quickly standing in the corner, frozen in fear. I told him we had to get out of there and grabbed his arm, but he yanked it away and told me that he was scared. I don't remember exactly what I said to get him to come, but it worked. I grabbed his arm again, and we ran out together just as the firefighters ran in.

As my brothers and I stood outside, we watched the flames come out the upstairs window. A few moments later, our mother arrived out of nowhere. Some would think her first response would have been are you all ok? But from what I remember, it was not. I remember her saying, "Oh, I'm about to beat y'all muthafucking asses!"

I remember how afraid I was at that moment, and I thought maybe I should ask a firefighter for help. I wanted to tell them she left us alone all the time, and we never had much food. I wanted them to take me away with them. Maybe they could at least tell her not to beat us. But I knew that wouldn't help; no one ever did and asking would only make it worse for me. The next thought I had was to make sure my brothers did not get in trouble for this. I had to protect them because this fire was not their fault. I put their lives in danger and had not thought about the consequences of what would happen because of my dumb decision.

The firefighters got the fire out, and we had only lost half of the top floor. They must have been close by because they wouldn't have been able to save the house had they not gotten there so quickly. My mom started my beating as the last fireman was leaving the house. I remember looking at him with sadness and disappointment because I thought they were supposed to be there to protect people. I felt he should have saved me.

That was one of the worst beatings I had ever gotten. I remember how angry my mom was. You could always tell the level of anger based on the carefulness of the beating and the selection of the weapon used against you. The weapon of choice this time was the extension cord from the phone. On a beating weapons scale from 1 – 10, I think the extension cord is a 10. It leaves lasting marks and maximum physical pain. The marks create a mental remembrance of that pain which is almost as hard as receiving it in the first place.

Regarding carefulness of the beating, that means the area of the body where the beating takes place. When we were getting a beating for something simple, we usually would take hits directly to the butt. But for severe problems like setting your house on fire, my whole body was open for punishment. As I have stated before, I am sure this is an example of the time; but I know I deserved all that I had coming to me. I had no one to blame but myself. I knew I was wrong and the seriousness of what I had done.

The question for me here is why? Why had I made such a dumb decision? Why had I not comprehended the consequences of such a reckless action? At the age of ten, I should have understood the gravity of this situation before it even started.

PART 3

THE TURNING

POINT

CHAPTER 20 | MOVING BACK

Around 1991 the decision was made to move from Joliet back to the Chicago area. We were excited to be going back home; going back to Summit was near family and some of our friends. We could go outside and be around more who knew us. We had spent so much time being left alone in the motels and our previous places it was a treat to have a home full of people. Being back made me feel better.

Being around people who didn't mistreat me meant the world to me. Even though we didn't have many nice things, there was constant love, protection, and a sense of belonging, which meant more to me than nice things ever could. I could tell that my siblings were in a better place mentally, just as I was.

My brothers and I had experienced many heartbreaks while away from Summit. Although we would still experience hardship, it would not be on the level as when we were in Joliet. In Summit, there was laughter and possibilities. There were people who would invite us into their homes where we would feel comfortable and sometimes even get fed.

I don't know what sparked the move, but I am sure it had something to do with my grandma making the same move just a few months earlier. Whatever the reason, we were happy about it.

My father's parents were also there, so we could see them more. My dad's mom loved us like crazy and would always want us to come to eat. She took care of her mother, who we thought was super mean. But as I grew up, I realized she just had high standards. If you were going to be around her, you just had to be respectful and do the right thing, or she did not want you around. As an adult, I've learned how important that was to see those standards set for me.

Me and my good friend Nick Mays

A great summer day in Summit, Argo

CHAPTER 21 | SEED PLANTING

I finished the 5th grade after we moved back to Summit. I was eleven years old. There I began to make a name for myself but only because I was causing trouble in school. We had moved into a two-bedroom apartment with my grandma, grandpa, uncle Edward, his girlfriend, and her son. My mom, sister, three younger brothers, and I made eleven people living in a small apartment. We still did not have much, but we were at least around family. There was love in this environment, and even in the cramped living space, I felt better.

I was growing up and coming into my own. The start of 6th grade would be an exciting year for me. Enthusiasm was high because I was going to be in middle school. I wasn't getting bullied as much, but that was because I didn't mind a good fight, and I had found out that I was pretty good at it. Most people are afraid of the pain of a fight and getting punched, but I discovered that my pain tolerance was pretty high.

Don't get me wrong. I was still fighting a lot, a few times a week on the bad weeks. A particular family in the neighborhood was always in the middle of neighborhood fights. So, most of the time, it was someone from that family with whom I and others in the hood would have problems. I think fighting them made me a little tougher as well. But mainly, I owed my toughness to my brother

Taiwan and my friend Mainee. I was the boss when we were left alone, and I took my job seriously, but Taiwan was a tough little boy who did not want to get bossed around. So we would fight it out pretty regularly. I would win every time, but he would always make me work for it. Taiwan is my right-hand man all the time now, and we will always be there to love and support each other.

Solidifying my toughness, my friend Mainee used to beat me up when we would fight. Whenever he would finally let me up, I would punch him again, and then he would grab me and beat me up some more. After a few minutes, he would ask me if I had enough, and I would say yes but always tried to strike again. I tell those two stories to help you understand why I did not mind a good fight, even if I knew I would lose.

The first day of school was right around the corner, and my mom had bought us something new to wear for our first day. Even though the things we had gotten had been cheap, they were new. I even got a few school supplies and a new book bag which had been on layaway for the whole summer. I was proud of this bookbag, and I was proud of my mom for doing what she had to do to get it for me. It was yellow with black straps, and it was perfect. I could not wait to show it off on the first day of school. As a kid with primarily second-hand items, it was everything I ever wanted.

We wanted to show up on the first day with something new like all the rest of the students. We did not want to be left out, feeling second-hand ourselves. We needed a fighting chance to fit in without being called out on day one by a teacher or a student for something that would embarrass us. That year since we did not smell foul or have on dirty clothes, we fit in like everyone else and made it through unnoticed for the first few days. We did not have the best, but we did not have the worst. Plus, everyone already knew who we were, and they knew we were not a family with a lot of money, so nobody expected name-brand things. That wasn't me anyway; I was never a name-brand type of kid. I preferred two new shirts from Walmart over one name-brand shirt.

I ran into my first problem during the second week of school. A bully that most people would not think was a problem. This girl's name was Stephanie, and she was about 6' feet tall. In my eyes, she was an unhinged crazy woman that walked around with no consideration for all of us smaller people. Again, I have no clue what I did to get under her skin, but I knew I would have to defend myself against her one day. I did not want to fight her for apparent reasons. One, she was a girl, and two, she was white. We all know a black boy or man doing anything to a white girl or woman never ends well. I had learned this lesson from my history lesson on Emmett Till and all the stories of black men having problems with white women.

To be smart about it, I spoke with a teacher about this girl. I told the teacher that this girl was calling me names, and when she would see me in the hallway, she would bump into me on purpose. She would always try to get a reaction out of me, and she wanted me to do something to get in trouble. I tried to take the correct route and tell the teachers so that I could have a good year. This was a new year for me and a chance to establish that I could be a good kid. I had been in multiple fights since arriving in Summit. I felt like most people wanted to see if I was as tough as my father was. People loved a good fighter, which drew many people in my direction. It did not worry me too much because it was just part of growing up in Chicago. As young men in the neighborhood, fighting was just a thing. After a good fight, the two kids involved would be back playing together with no problems. Plus, my name carried a lot of weight because of who my father was. So some of those fights came because of his name.

I was kicked out of one school for fighting, sent to another, and placed in special education. Everyone had already labelled me a 'bad' kid, and teachers had no idea what to do with me. I understand I misbehaved, but I was also respectful. I would fight only when someone would pick on me. I never wanted to fight and never would start them. I wanted to be the kid everyone liked, not the kid known for being dirty or fighting in class. But that reputation followed me everywhere I went, no matter how much I wanted it to be different.

Although sixth grade had started decently, the next few weeks were tough. Everything about the school was awful. I had started to get bullied again more and more. As I explained in earlier chapters, once you are labelled as the kid that could be picked on, the door is open for anyone who wants to try. I knew this, but I was going to make sure this did not happen at this school. I was done with being that kid, and I was going to show everyone that I was not the one to mess with anymore, or there would be consequences.

My home life was not the greatest, but it was getting better because we had a place to live, and there were people that I loved and who loved me. With the newfound peace at home, I was also trying to achieve that at school. Accomplishing this would be difficult because even after speaking with teachers, I could find no help. I figured I had to attack my problems head-on and not run from the bullies.

I went to school on a Monday with the mindset that whoever wanted to pick on me and fight would get it. If someone wanted to pick on me or make fun of me, we could fight right now and get it over with. I entered the school building feeling good and ready to take on the world. I was 5' 5 and 100 pounds, but I was walking with my chest out and my chin up. I was on a mission to set the record straight.

As I was strutting down the crowded hall feeling good about myself, someone stepped on the back of my shoe. It ripped off the back half of the already tattered sole of my shoe. I was instantly upset, and all the confidence I had seconds earlier melted away. I looked up just in time to see Stephanie walking toward me.

She had an odd dragging walk where one of her legs would almost shuffle behind her. That odd shuffle was probably why she was such a terrible bully. She knew it was better to be the biggest bully than to get bullied herself.

It was too late to run, so there was nothing to do but prepare for whatever was coming. Everyone around seemed to notice she was coming for me and stopped to watch the show. Sure enough, she did not disappoint and pushed me so damn hard that I hit the lockers. I could feel the handle of the locker smash into my back. She kept walking as I crashed and fell, so I stood up and yelled, "You fat bitch!" The crowd roared with surprise, but that also caused her to be embarrassed, so she knew she would have to respond. She yelled, "I bet you won't say that shit outside?"

Everyone looked back at me to see what my response would be. I was stuck, so I paused. I thought she would kill me right there, but she turned and walked away. As she turned the corner, I started to get brave again, so I yelled, "I bet I will!" She had already turned the corner, so she did not hear me. But I believed since I said something that helped me save face in front of all who were looking and listening.

The end of the day had arrived, and it was time to walk home. As soon as I walked out of the classroom, I saw a crowd of kids waiting to ensure I went in the correct direction. At that moment, I knew it would go down today. I went to my locker to grab my stuff, including the brand-new book bag that my mom bought for me—the bag that was on layaway all summer, the one I was so proud of having.

As I got to my locker, I could hear all the students talking about me getting ready to fight, as if I wasn't even there. Someone came up to me and asked me if I was scared. I don't remember what I said back to them. I want to think I denied being scared, but I doubt it. I heard someone say she was right outside the door. I was terrified, but I had to play it cool. I didn't want it to seem like I was the one that started the fight.

I stared forward as I walked past her, but she swiped my bookbag, knocking it off my shoulder and onto the ground. I don't know what came over me, but that did it. That was the trigger I needed. I immediately turned and punched her in the stomach. Then I struck her in the face as quickly as possible before some people grabbed me. That was it, I had just beat up the school bully, and it felt great, and everyone was cheering me on.

I felt like I was on top of the world. As we walked home, everyone talked about the fight and how I looked like the character from Mike Tyson's game Punch Out. I was the little guy fighting the giant person. I was reveling in all the attention as the hero and took pride in that gift because it was not often given to me.

On the walk home, the adrenaline had subsided. I started to think about everything that had just happened. To be honest, I felt horrible. I felt terrible for beating someone up but awful because she was a girl. That was the first time in my life and the last time I hit a woman. I felt like I should have done more to prevent the fight because she was a girl. But I made excuses of why I thought it was the right thing to do the whole way home. I told myself it was ok because she was bigger than me and the aggressor. She was a bully, and everyone wanted me to do it, which made it acceptable. While at home with space and time to think, I realized how dumb the decision had been to fight her. I knew I would have to learn how to control myself better. Self-control had become a massive problem for me at this time in my life.

The following day we got to school, and I was immediately called to the front office by the principal. I tried to explain that she had been bullying me and hitting me for about two weeks, but the principal didn't care. The only punishment we received for the incident was that we had to eat lunch in the principal's office for a week. Since we had gotten in trouble, I thought everything would be ok now. I thought our beef was over, but that was not the case. Being in trouble did not scare her at all.

Even with us being in the principal's office, she was still a bully. While we were eating in the principal's office, if she saw something on my tray that she wanted, she would take it. She was making fun of my clothes, my bad haircuts, the fact that I was poor, and anything else that she could think would hurt me. One day, she stood up and slapped me before taking my lunch. She sat down to start eating, and I was so angry. About five minutes later, I stood up behind her with my tray and hit her across the back of her head with it.

Of course, I got caught in my retaliation. I got paddled five times and received a few extra days of eating lunch alone in the principal's office. After that I was furious! I felt bad about beating her up and disrespecting her as a girl. But after all the time in the office together, she still treated me terribly. As much as I had regretted the fight after it happened, I didn't feel bad about it anymore. My hatred for her had grown. It had grown to the point where I wished she was dead. I was sure our paths were going to have to cross again soon.

One thing about being a little black boy in America is that we never seem to get a break. We must always deal with situations that prevent us from being typical kids.

As I was dealing with the Stephanie situation, another bully named Jesse wanted to ignite some made-up beef he had with me. I cannot tell you what sparked our problem. I have no clue why he did not like me or why he had decided to pick on me. I was reaching the end of my rope with these people bullying me, and I felt I was about to lose it. I knew I had to do something to stop it once and for all.

When you are the small, poor kid that is not the smartest, you become an easy target. That kid was me. Jesse was a little different because he was a boy, and I didn't feel bad if I had to fight him, but I was trying not to get in a lot of trouble. People at school had already talked about me needing to go to an alternative school for students with bad behavior. I was desperately trying to avoid going to the school known as PRIDE. It was a step below a juvenile detention center. I can't remember what it stood for, but the bad disruptive students got sent there, and I'll say it mostly consisted of young black boys.

Once in this school, you could not get out unless you worked your way up some stupid level system. And not many kids were ever able to work themselves out of this school. Most students that ended up going to this place would be there until they graduated high school. If I ended up at this school, there would be no prom, no sports, and no freedom to walk the halls with my friends. You were not even allowed to walk to the restrooms by yourself. In my eyes, you might as well be in jail or juvenile detention. So, fighting Jesse was not one of my top options. I tried to stay away from him and keep my head down. One day our paths crossed and what I had tried to avoid for so long was now imminent.

One day as the bell rang, hundreds of kids rushed the halls like always. As we all fought to get to our classes, someone bumped me hard. I looked back, and it was Jesse. We were now face to face, he was talking crap, and although I was trying to prevent a fight from breaking out right there, I was still talking crap right back at him. That confrontation did not turn physical, but it did encourage him to set up a fight for after school.

There I was, stuck again. I could not avoid this, and I could not run home. One of the worst things you could do in the hood was run away from a fight. Then you would be called a chicken, coward, or worse, all words you wanted to avoid. Once you get labeled a coward, things would get even more challenging for you. So, it was on, the fight was set for after school, and I had to go. The only issue with this was that I had plans to take care of something else after school.

I had to deal with someone else that had taken things a little too far, and I was going to make them pay. If I could just put this problem off for a couple of days, maybe I would not have to deal with it at all. My plan would change my reputation and probably prevent the fight with Jesse altogether. The bell rang; I retrieved my things and then headed to the back of the school. This walk was different because I knew I was going there to fight; there would be no way of avoiding it. I could feel the crowd of people walking behind and next to me. Escorting me to the ring like I'm a lightweight champion.

As we reached the back of the school, I had to climb over a piece of wood that poetically seemed to represent my climb into a boxing ring. Once I entered the ring, I had a quick mental reminder of what I had to do after this fight. Was I romanticizing what I had planned? Was I excited about it or scared? Anyways I focused back on the task at hand, which was the boxing match with Jesse. All I knew was, I better win this, or he will be a problem all year. Who am I fooling? If we get in trouble for this fight,

I will probably get kicked out of this school. But I had no choice but to fight. The best I could hope for was a win, and because it was outside of the school, no teachers would find out.

Here I am, standing face to face with Jesse; we both waited to see who would make the first move—staring at each other, talking, telling each other to swing. I stood there contemplating if I should slap him, push him, or if I'm going to bite him once I got him down.

Time was ticking, and I had to do something fast because I was running out of time to make it to my other big plan. I thought that whatever I did, I had to establish that I was not the one to keep messing with. I even thought for a moment I would pull my knife out and stab him if I had to. I quickly took that option off the table because that would get me in way more trouble than I needed.

But whatever I did, I had to establish the precedent that he didn't want to fight me. I had to do something extreme and memorable. I knew I needed to strike first, so I pulled my arm back with my fist as tight as possible and swung. The first blow connected to his face and then another that I don't remember where it landed. Being smaller, I had extended too far, and I caused myself to be off-balance. As I tried to regain my balance, I saw his fist coming for my face. I felt the pain as he landed his punch;

I wanted to get him to the ground so I could bite him, but he was too big to get down. So, we both continued to swing and grab, and then he lost his balance this time. I knew he was going down, so I tried to assist him with a good kick.

As he was stumbling towards the ground while trying to catch himself, something happened that I didn't plan on. Jesse hit the ground and then was screaming and swinging but not towards me. I then noticed what everyone that was watching had seen. His arm had fallen under him, and it was all twisted up and mangled. Everyone was yelling and pointing at his arm.

Once I saw how bad it looked, I knew I was in big trouble. I helped him up off the ground and walked him to the office. I begged him to say we were playing around the whole way, but he didn't. Instead of sitting there waiting to get in trouble, I got up and got out of that building as fast as I could.

I could not stay around much longer because I had big plans for that day. This was the day I had decided to get rid of my biggest problem for good. This was the day that would change my life and my reputation. But I did not know that breaking another kid's arm would be what would save my life and change the direction of my family's legacy.

CHAPTER 22 | CATCHING A BODY

I can remember running full speed down the street. I knew I was late because of the fight with Jesse. With tunnel vision, I could see nothing but my location and myself taking the shot. I had to put everything else out of my head if I was going to be able to do this.

I could no longer think of anything else and felt numb. It felt as if I was outside of my body, jogging right behind, watching, and feeling the same feelings that my body was feeling. I was able to use my sense of sight and the emotional gravity of the situation. I saw nervousness and fear and felt the sweating and shakiness. My clouded eyes and the desert-like feeling in my mouth caused an unforgettable look on my face. It's as if I wanted to laugh now and cry later, or maybe do both simultaneously.

I wanted to reach out and grab the little boy who was about to make this terrible mistake and hug him while he cried in my arms. I wanted to tell him that he did not have to do this and that everything would be ok. I reached out to grab him as he jogged, but it didn't work. I could not stop him. I could not talk any sense into him. I do not think I had ever told him how much I loved him. Self-love was not something spoken about much in our household.

I tried to get all of the noise in my head to shut off and only think about pulling this cold trigger. I had never shot this gun before, others yes, but this one no, not yet, today would be the day. I was nervous and scared, and I felt terrible already. I thought of the family and how sad they would be. Then I snapped out of it and thought about how much pain I had experienced, how much embarrassment I had felt. I had been pushed over the edge because it was going on far too long.

Being bullied made me feel like I wanted to take my own life sometimes, and I did not want any more of those thoughts. I thought someone needed to pay for causing me to feel like this. I was so angry but trying to keep myself calm. I got to the spot, and I looked around to see if anyone had seen me run back here.

I was in the clear. Some of the kids were still walking home. I could hear their happiness and laughter, which made me even madder because I wished I had that. I am still sweating, but I am trying to get it under control. I knew it was almost time. I checked to make sure the gun was ready to go. I pulled a ski mask out of my black and yellow book bag and placed it over my face. The first thing I thought was, this feels too hot! I laughed at myself because I wondered if the killers on TV ever felt this way. Yes, I knew this was not a good time to make jokes, but it popped into my head.

Once my mask was on, I took my shirt off, put my bookbag on my shoulder and then put my shirt back on. I did this so that my shirt would cover my bag and my hands could be free. I did not want to be like the people on TV and hold the gun with one hand and then miss the shot. I was looking down the street as all the kids were coming closer. I see the group of kids that Stephanie usually walked with. They were some of her friends that would always laugh when she bullied me.

I rechecked my mask and checked the gun. I can see them, and they are getting closer. My heart felt like it was beating a thousand beats a minute, and I started to shake uncontrollably. As the kids walked by, I held the gun up and waited to pull the trigger. The fear was gone. I better not miss this shot. I was ready to do what I had to do. I was prepared to jump out and shoot as each of her friends walked by.

The last person walked by, and it was not Stephanie. Where had she gone? I was livid and ripped the mask off as I stood there, disappointed and confused. Honestly, I do not know how I felt about missing this opportunity. I do not know if I even wanted to do it. I thought I had to, but what would have happened if I did? It was that damn fight with Jesse that made me miss my chance. I was stuck thinking if I should try again, or was this a sign? Was this a missed opportunity, or was this God saving my life? Better yet, was this God saving my soul?

CHAPTER 23 | TURNING POINT

After the failed attempt to shoot Stephanie, I returned to school wondering why she had not walked the same path home that she did every day. I was left wondering and would never find out because I was called to the office before I could even start my investigation into what went wrong.

Over the loudspeaker, a voice said, "Chucky Davis to the principal office." Immediately the whole class starts in on me, "Oh, you in trouble. You broke Jesse's arm and you 'bout to get kicked out of school." I could hear all the laughing as I got up, grabbed my bag, and walked out of the classroom.

Sure enough, I was absolutely in trouble. I was suspended for five days and never returned to that school again. During that five-day suspension, the school and my mom had a meeting. At this point, I had been kicked out of every elementary school I had attended. Because of this, I could not go to any other middle schools in my district. They deemed I had too many behavior problems and learning difficulties to remain in a typical school setting.

They thought it was best for me to be placed in a school that would better serve my needs in a small group setting. Somewhere that could help control my behavior issues. As a special education student in that era, I lacked a lot of the academic support afforded to students in school today. I don't remember a single IEP meeting for a plan to help me catch up to the other students. I think I became such a problem for most teachers that they would pass me to get me out of their class and on to the next teacher. They did not care, as long as I was not their problem anymore.

And that was it. My worst fear was realized. The last option for me before juvenile detention was an alternative school. The name of this school was PRIDE, located in Oak Lawn, Illinois. So, the day came when it was time for me to return to school, it was a new school with new people, and I was 12 years old.

The first thing that came to mind was who would I have to fight first. The school was about 30 minutes from my house, so I rode the bus. Well, the school's transportation was a 1993 Chevrolet Suburban. They had a parking lot full of them that they would dispatch out around the communities and pick up bad kids who had gotten kicked out of their regular schools. There were usually about 6 to 8 kids on each bus.

I started my time at PRIDE as a sixth-grade middle schooler and finished the rest of my sixth-grade year there. At first, it started a little shaky. I did not like many teachers or the students. I think it was because I was in a new environment, a new building, and getting to know people all over again.

We had two teachers in each class then we would have a rec time. During rec time, we could play pool, ping-pong, board games, and even go to the school store, which had snacks we could purchase with reward money that we could earn from being good in class. That was a motivational tool the school used that many of us were excited about. We would eat lunch in the rec room and then go to the school store for snacks.

It was a small class setting, so there were never more than ten kids in a class. That helped a lot to get one-on-one help from the teacher whenever we needed it. Also, having two teachers in the class prevented fights from breaking out. Once or twice a week, each student would have to see a counselor, which I hated initially. But after a while, I didn't mind because she was very pretty and I used to love going to see her. Her name was Lisa, and throughout my time there, she probably was my favorite person in the school building.

All the kids in the school had some form of behavior issues and academic problems, but mainly it was a behavior problem that got us all sent to the school. While I was there, I had a tough time adjusting. They were on a chart system where the better you did in class, the higher you would move up on their chart system; once you reached level eight, you could go back to your regular school. However, many people graduated from PRIDE because they could never get themselves in control enough to be admitted back into their home school.

I was one of the kids who struggled my first year. I did not listen to the teachers and didn't want to do any schoolwork. I was so angry that I had to be at the school with these new people and ride in the Suburban. I was very self-conscious about the people of my neighborhood watching that Suburban pick me up every day and knowing I was in the alternative school.

During my time at PRIDE, I experienced some students who had huge racism problems, and quite often, they used the "n" word in front of me. That was always upsetting, so then I would fight. I had always tried to be a kid who did the right thing, and I never fought just for the sake of fighting or because I liked it. I didn't like fighting, but I was good at it. I was pushed to that brink quite often, and the school's goal was to get students to control their anger and not always revert to fighting as their escape route.

That concept was challenging for me to accept because growing up, all I knew was if someone does something to you, disrespects you, or hits you, you fight them every time they do it to make sure that they don't do it again. While trying not to fight, my anger would turn to

185

rage. The teachers would tell me to calm down and then take me to speak to the counselor. I spent a lot of time with the counselor because of my anger issues.

One time it was this blind kid named Chris. He wasn't 100% blind, but he did require using a walking stick. Chris was very annoying, and sometimes when we'd be in the hallway, Chris would hit people in their legs with his walking stick. We all knew that Chris would do this on purpose sometimes because he knew he could get away with it. On this day, as we walked down the hall in a single file line. Chris was at the end of the line behind me. Chris hit my feet with his stick, I turned around and asked him not to do it, and he said, "Ok, sorry."

We continued walking down the hall, and again he hit me, in my legs this time. I didn't ask nicely this time as I said to Chris, "Don't hit me with your stick again, or I'm gonna kick your ass." I turn back around, and Chris hits me with the stick again. At this point, I was torn in between if I should tell the teacher or if I should kick the crap out of Chris. I did not want to fight Chris because he was blind, which felt unfair, but on the other hand, I truly believed that he knew what he was doing.

Continuing to the rec room, Chris hits me with a stick again, and I lose it. I felt Chris was being disrespectful and taking advantage of his disability, so I did what I thought I should. I turned around and punched Chris in the face twice. He fell to the ground, and I got on top of him and started hitting him again. The teacher ran up and yelled 'staff,' which was the word they used during a fight. All the teachers ran down the hall to break up the fight and restrain the participants.

One of the teachers picked me up as high as he could, body-slammed me face-first into the floor, pulled my arms behind my back, and pushed my wrists as high towards my neck as they would stretch. I began to scream because it was painful. Then another teacher came and firmly pressed her knee in my back until I calmed down. That day, I learned a valuable lesson: do not be rude or beat up the blind kid. Teachers do not like that.

After the fight, they immediately took me to see the counselor, where she probed my brain to figure out why I thought it was ok to fight the blind kid. I told her it was simple, he was disrespectful, and he kept hitting me with his stick. I could not understand why no one understood that he was hitting me first, and I thought that was a legitimate reason to hit him back. In my opinion, I was being an equal opportunity jerk to treat everybody fairly.

The first year was rough, but I began to settle in because of the counselor. I genuinely believe I would have been dead by now if it weren't for my counseling. I was a danger to those who bothered me, and because of my intrusive thoughts, I was a danger to myself. I had many incidents where I had thought about ending my life or taking someone else's. That is a lot of torment for a kid only in the sixth grade. During my time at PRIDE, I learned how to cope with my anger and mistreatment by others. Also, to let go of the anger, I felt because of not having the things I thought I deserved. I learned a great deal about accepting help from teachers that I did not believe had my best interest at hand.

My primary teacher, Linda, was very harsh on me, and I despised her then. I was disrespectful to her every chance I got. But I see now she was harsh on me because of the attitude I gave, and I wouldn't have liked me then either.

Because of PRIDE's level system, I learned how to accept responsibility for my actions. I learned how to trust others and show others that I was trustworthy and could be accountable for my actions. I was taught how to speak up for myself when I felt I was being wronged and how to express my anger without fighting.

There, I learned how to play sports and be a good team player. I also learned how to study and focus, and it was all because of the small group atmosphere. Because the classrooms were not filled with thirty or more kids, teachers could give me the quality time that I needed to understand the lessons they were teaching in class. Overall, the school was a total package for me. I finally had mental and academic support and steady discipline. The teachers supported me and did not pass me off to the next to get rid of me.

There were a few hiccups here and there. I started my own gang at that school. Because of this, I got kicked out of the regular classroom setting for two weeks, and they separated the kids who were a part of it. I've always wanted to do the right thing, so even within this gang, I controlled the class and didn't allow people to fight without permission. I even implemented strict rules about not being disrespectful to teachers. Kids were not allowed to be disrespectful to teachers, or they would have to suffer the consequences.

There was an order in the classroom, and when we went to lunch. I thought the gang was good since there was less trouble in our classes and the students respected the teachers. If they tried to act up in class, I would prevent it with my right-hand man, Farris. He was a big Arabic kid, and it was his idea to bring in a five-point star with all our names on it. But that little gang didn't last long, probably for the best.

I began to work my way up the levels while controlling my temper and doing my classwork. I understood the system in my seventh and eighth grade school year at Pride. By the time I was in eighth grade, I had loved school, and there wasn't one teacher in the building that I did not love. I respected them all, and they all respected me. They had seen me grow from sixth grade to eighth grade. They watched me start as a troublemaker and become a respectful student who didn't fight much anymore. I became a kid who could control himself and his temper and be accountable for his mistakes.

I want to contribute most of that personal growth to my counselor, Lisa. Her guidance was the contributing factor to the confidence that I had built in myself. That set the tone for what I wanted to do next year. With all that confidence that I had created, I knew next year that I wanted something different in life. Eighth grade is when I started to plant the seed in my brain that I would change my circumstances. I was going to be better than what my environment had shown me.

Eighth grade is when I knew I wanted better for my life and my family. I knew I wanted to be someone important someday, with a good-paying job and a big house. I had earned the trust of my teachers, and I did my work in school and at home. I even began gaining my mother's trust, and I stopped smoking weed, no more drinking, and no gang banging at all.

Next year I was going to be in high school, and I felt I had outgrown PRIDE. I decided it was time to be a better version of myself. It was time for me to show the world the new me. I knew I had the tools to be better than I used to be. I had a support group, and I was focused.

I decided that I was going to play football and go to college. I had never before even considered going to college. I thought long and hard about my plan to set my goals and create my turning point. I knew what I had to do, and nothing was going to stop me from reaching that goal. I decided that I wanted better for myself, which was the number one thing that drove me. I no longer wanted to be poor. I did not want to be dumb. I did not want to go to jail, and I did not want to die on the streets.

At that time, I had decided that I wanted to live my life, and I wondered if I could be better than people ever thought I could. I wanted to invest in myself and begin working to change my family's legacy. I vowed to carry the Davis name to new heights. I felt that I had all the tools I needed to start, I knew I would have to learn and work to gain more knowledge, but I had what was required to begin my journey.

So that is what I did. I began implementing all the lessons I had learned in my short time on this planet. I began to think about what rules I would have to live by to reach the goals I wanted to achieve. I knew to be the man I wanted to become, I had to put God first. I remember my grandma telling me that nothing is possible without God.

CHAPTER 24 |EYES WIDE CLOSED

When did I realize my turning point? When I thought I should shoot my bully? Possibly, when I was tied to a pole in a basement for days or maybe the time, I was forced to do a drive-by shooting that I did not want to do.

You would think those horrific situations were when I should have realized my turning point. You would think that at the end of one of those horrible situations is when I said to myself, Charles, it's time for you to do better. Any of those situations could have been the moment but guess what, they were not. For some reason, it just did not click in my mind at any of those times. The moment came when I yelled at a teacher for trying to help me, cursed her out, and called her every bad name I could think of for a white woman.

I decided that this moment had to be the time of my turning point because that same teacher pulled me to the side after the terrible things I had just said to her. She told me, "I don't care what anyone else says about you, you are special, and you have the ability to be great. I will not let you self-destruct on my watch, and I will not give up on you. You can be great if and when you decide you are ready to be great. You can turn a corner."

I couldn't believe that after all the stuff I said to her, all the names I had called her, all the times I was terrible in this woman's class, this teacher called me to the side and said I am not giving up on you. She told me, "You can call me all the names you want to. I'm still going to love you, and I'm still going to be there to help you be great." In honor of her, I use the phrase 'Turning Point.'

Her words stayed with me for days, but they didn't hit me immediately. I was a little pissed and thought, who does she think she is? She doesn't know me, and I can't be great, I can't graduate middle school, and I definitely can't get through high school. Who is this white lady selling me these fake dreams? I was angry and bitter and didn't have anything or anyone, or so I thought at the time, but honestly, there were good people in my life always trying to get me to do the right thing. But my mind was not picking up what they were handing out. I couldn't relate to the message they were trying to deliver because of the packaging it was in. It was wrapped and entangled in toughness. My mind was not accepting toughness.

After so much trauma, my mind required a different type of love and teaching. Until then, it seemed as if people were just barking at me, and because of this, I would just shut down. Then I decided to be the one to do the barking.

I had assumed that everyone in an authority position was out to bark at me, so I programmed myself to bark first. But what this teacher did to me was she took my horrible and negative energy and decided not to match me. She decided to take it and kill me with kindness. She delivered a package of love, honesty, and caring. I do not know how or why, but I finally received it. I received it like never before.

I thought about what the teacher had said all night. The next day I was embarrassed to go to her class because I had acted like such a jerk the day before. I could not believe she had laid that load of positive words on me. I looked around at my environment and my whole life and situation. I was embarrassed by who I was and knew it was time for me to change.

I started to analyze what I had been doing and the situations I had been putting myself in. That teacher's words made me look at myself, and only then did I start thinking about the future. She made me wonder if I could genuinely have one. I had never had this feeling before and didn't know what it was. It was such a new concept that it felt strange and foreign. I thought I might rebel against it, shake it off, or get it out of me.

So often, people who are not used to positive behavior do not know how to accept it once it is introduced. As much as I tried to get it away from me, I couldn't. I could not shake it; she had implanted the seed in my mind. The feelings and thoughts were moving through my body, forcing themselves to grow despite my effort to remove them. Her words had attached themselves to me, and I was obsessed with the thought of becoming something great. I could graduate high school, go to college, and be great. I kept feeding it. These thoughts I kept playing in my head acted as the water needed to grow the seed.

How did this happen? Who have I become? My eyes were open, and I started to see things differently. I had begun to believe that I could be somebody. I heard those words before, but why have such an impact now? Was it the messenger? Was it the package it was delivered in? I was confused, but now I had a taste for the images in my head. I wanted to experience greatness. I had made the decision and started seeing things I hadn't seen before. I saw positivity. I saw the students that did well in school and fathers taking care of their families. I saw parents working hard and raising their kids.

I would go places and observe people at the register paying for something without thinking about how much it cost. I saw families in a nice home, laughing together, kids getting gifts for Christmas under a big, beautifully decorated tree. These images were implanted in my brain because of the seeds that the teacher had given me. I saw things I wanted and knew I could achieve them. This became my why!

It is within you to find your turning point and what your why is. Now that I knew why I wanted a better life, it was time to figure out how. How am I going to get these things? So, I started to ask the right questions. Some studies show if you ask a question, your mind has no choice but to wonder about it and try to find the answer. How do I get there?

Starting where I am right now, what would I have to do to graduate middle school? Then what do I need to do to graduate high school and potentially get into college? I started to map out what I needed to do to reach the images of the life I wanted to have. And I had the perfect plan to accomplish all I wanted using DAPPA. This idea would change my life.

CHAPTER 25 | THE MESSAGE

For you, Youth:

I have seen in the darkness of some terrible situations, often thinking that I would be better off dead. I have fought through that darkness and forced myself to witness the power of change. I strived for the kind of change that one can only dream about. I have been knocked down more times than I can count. But there is a promise on the other side of being knocked down. There is a promise on the other side of deciding to do great things with your life. There is a promise on the side of discipline and commitment. How committed do you want to be, and how much are you willing to give up to realize your turning point?

What are you willing to give up to exchange darkness for the light of excellence? That is a question that only you can answer. You must wholeheartedly want it and let go of the threads holding you back. You either decide to sacrifice for greatness, or you do not. As a younger person, I always wanted better deep down inside, but sometimes I just could not catch a break. The pressures that were on my back were said to be expected. Everyone has pressures, but they are more challenging when you want to do better and be better than the life you have been handed. Sometimes life beats you down so hard that you just expect that to be your everyday life.

I am writing to tell you that you must stay in the fight. You must understand that you cannot surrender to the norm that surrounds you daily. You are capable of so much more; you just have to believe and see your turning point. You have to discover your why and always remember to place that up against any situation you encounter.

There are going to be some tough days, and there are going to be some painful days. There will be days when you are abused, mentally and physically. But I say to you, stay strong, and please do not ever give up. You just have to trust someone to help you, but they are right in front of you. Even when it is hard to ask, you have to pull yourself to the point and just ask. I know what you are thinking. That's easy for you to say. I used to feel like this all the time. I used to think that my family needed me; I didn't want to get my parents in trouble, and I didn't want to be embarrassed for asking for help. I will guide you on how to find and reach your turning point. I will guide you through the steps that helped me accomplish the goals I had always dreamed of and how I changed my family's legacy for the better.

CHAPTER 26 | D.A.P.P.A

Many factors come along with seeing and creating your turning point. The first thing is accountability, which entails accepting responsibility for your actions. Not everything was my fault when I was younger. However, there were many situations that I could have chosen not to put myself into. I just made the wrong decision even when I could have done better. Why did I make some of those choices, I often ask myself? I often found a way to relate it to being someone else's fault. But when I take it a step further, I have to remind myself that only I am in control of my brain and actions. So even if there are consequences to not doing something, I still ultimately have the choice to do it or not. That is the decision. There lies the strength of decision-making.

Within that process, we have to understand that you must establish confidence before you can ever make an unpopular decision. A kid lacking confidence will likely make their decisions solely to be seen as cool or following the majority. Another major factor is the pressure of loyalty, many decisions will be made based on loyalty, but you must determine if the dedication is detrimental to your own well-being. If it is, then does that person or situation, you are making a wrong decision for deserve your loyalty when you are sacrificing yourself for it.

1. Decide
2. Accept
3. Plan
4. Prepare
5. Achieve

DECIDE- You have to decide to put in the work to be different. No one is going to give it to you. No one will be in the corner of someone unwilling to believe in themselves.

ACCEPT- I do not want this to sound harsh, but at some points, we have to call a spade a spade. You must learn to accept the circumstances you were born into. By accepting, you take back the power to override them. You are where you are because of the environment you were brought up in and/or the decisions you made to put yourself there. But you do not have to be a product of your environment, and you can change what you choose.

Before all significant changes, there must be a moment in time when you say; this is who I want to be and what I want my life to be like. Now that you have established this, what will you do about it? You have accepted your circumstances, but now you can change them. Ask yourself right now, who do you think you are? Say it out loud, "I am _____!" When I ask myself that question, my answer is I am unstoppable, brave, a great father, a hard worker, and a king. I am rich, proud, successful, and handsome. I am capable of everything I put my mind to and then work to achieve.

I hate to say it but putting your mind to something only gives you the dream. But when you put work into something, it gives you results! If you are poor, accept that that is where you are, but you will change it. If you are in jail, accept that is where you are, but you will do better when you get out. If you are not doing well in classes, accept that is where you are, but you will start doing better. Not later, not on Monday, not next year. Now! Your turning point should always start now! You are who you are but can become who you want to be right now.

PLAN- In the planning process, you have to ask yourself what it will take to make the changes you want in your life. What things will you have to change? What will you have to give up? During the change process, you will win some and lose some. Giving up things is usually the hard part that most have trouble accepting.

It's bizarre how in situations that are so damaging and horrible, we still find ourselves comfortable in them and uncomfortable making a change to get away from them. We know things are toxic for us. Our hearts are telling us that we need to leave and get out of this situation, but our minds are telling us that we might not be able to adjust, so we need to stay in the lane we know. Understand what is toxic in your life so you know what you need to change. Set your plan to remove yourself from those situations and be strong enough to implement and stick with that plan.

PREPARE- Setbacks will be a difficult part of this process that you will have to deal with consistently. They will be a regular part of your life but, with perseverance, can be overcome. There will be times during this journey when things will not go as planned, and you must prepare for the setbacks. Times will come that you will be discouraged. No one who has ever embarked on a life-changing experience has done so without setbacks. But you have to remember that you are doing something great. Something that possibly no one in your family or circle has ever done before. You have to go into it and understand that it will not be easy. But you have committed to seeing it through.

You have to remember what your "Why" is. Why do you want to make this change, and who are you doing it for? All of these questions have to be used as motivational tools. No one can force you to see or reach for your turning point. You must have the mindset that you have had enough and are hungry for a different life. I got to that point many times and always told myself I was tired of the situation. But guess what I did all those times? Not a single thing. I lived in my misery because I could not see the bigger picture. I could not see the light at the end of the tunnel. I had no book to read that would guide me through the process of improving my life. I needed a smoke signal to guide me through the steps and the process.

But most importantly, I needed the mental strength to decide to want better for myself and my family. I needed the courage to leave the toxic people, things, and situations alone. When I finally found that courage, my life flourished. I made strides toward being a better student, brother, son, and overall person. Once I did that, I started to see my way through the forest. I could see the light and understand the path that would lead me out of the darkness.

ACHIEVE- The fifth step in this process is to achieve! You have to work to be better than where you are today. Nothing in this world stays the same. You are either getting better or worse. You are getting worse every second you wait to put your plan into action. You are creating an even deeper ditch to dig yourself out of. Throughout my life, I have never been afraid of hard work, and if I decided to do something, I would do it 100%. Before my turning point, that work was robbing people, breaking into homes, and selling drugs, but it did it at 100%. But those things didn't get me very far.

When I decided to change my life, it became football training, getting through college, reaching million-dollar sales value in real estate, and selling my artwork. I would grind every day at 100% until I achieved whatever goal I had set for myself. No one could stop me once I had made up my mind about something. Once I made the honest decision that I wanted to reach the goal that my family would never want for anything in their lives. I hit the ground running, not looking back until I accomplished that goal.

Once I achieved that goal, I returned to my drawing board and prepared for the next one. Why? Because I knew I could do more and become even greater. I stopped blaming others, took accountability for my actions and mistakes, and went at my goals hard. Why not get my Master's degree and PhD? Why not write a best-selling book about my journey in life? How many kids just like me can I help find their turning points? This mentality separates me from other people. I will not allow anyone to outwork me. Also, I am not afraid to ask for help or advice.

I built a strong foundation of people around me who were more intelligent than me. People who have accomplished some of their goals before me. People who may have even been in the same field as me. I watched, studied, and I learned. To be successful, you can't be afraid to ask for assistance. Stack your circle with people who are like-minded and build you up. Again, remember there will be setbacks, but remember your end goal and remind yourself how bad you want it. Understand the consequences if you do not make the needed changes in your life. Understand the circumstances you say you are willing to accept if you don't make the changes. Just remember this is your life, and you must set the changes in motion and work every day to make them your reality. You have to help yourself first before you can help anyone else. Actions speak louder than words, but results scream I made it!

CHAPTER 27 | BROKEN BOY

Why does the broken boy dream?

He dreams because he is free.

He is unbothered, he is rich, and sometimes poor.

But happy because he doesn't want for anything more.

He dreams because he can free others.

He dreams because he has joy, and he is unharmed.

The broken boy dreams because he is protected.

He dreams because he goes unmolested.

He justifies his thoughts,

By criticizing his faults.

A forced effort to memorize his heart.

Still, he is broken by all means,

Yet still he dreams.

He dreams because in that place he can be

Everything that he dreams.

It's simple.

The broken boy dreams simply because it

Makes him whole again.

So, he dreams.

—C.Davis

CHAPTER 28 | S.I.R.

Teachers and Mentors:

The desired journey for you is to open your eyes to the misunderstood kid sitting in front of you with hunger pains. The pains were experienced because some nights, I would not eat to ensure my brothers would have enough to get full. Also, the realization that your words, no matter how insignificant you may think, can make or break your possibility of forming a positive relationship with a student. I specifically remember a teacher who was a white woman that I overheard say the "n" word within earshot of us kids. This single moment ruined my relationship with that teacher. You must never forget that your words have so much power. They have the power to give, or they have the power to take.

Possibly, you have a child that sits in your class with a terrible attitude and refuses to read aloud or answer questions. I did that as a child, but only because I feared the words jumping around on the page and getting confused because my ability to read was nonexistent.

You could be the teacher, neighbor, social worker, or even foster parent who has recognized these problems with children in your classrooms, neighborhoods, and homes who are desperate to help but unsure how to start. With that, I hope this can give each of you the insight you might need to make a difference in the lives of those children.

While reading these stories of my childhood, some may have felt bad for me, at times you did not like me, and you may even think of me as the villain because of the truths of my life. However, with everything I went through as a child, I can now see the positive attributes born out of my darkness. To my surprise, a group of extraordinary teachers pulled me out of my darkness and despair one step at a time.

Many of us forget about the critical role a positive teacher can play in a young child's life who has no one else to turn to. These select few teachers saved my life. They prevented me from taking my life on more than one occasion, and I will always hold a special place in my heart for these teachers. They are why I chose to become a teacher myself, to share that knowledge and use my experiences to help as many children as possible.

Although this book is about my life, it cannot be complete without accurately depicting the life-changing gestures from so many great people inside and outside the classroom that played a role in saving my life. I would love to go back and tell my teachers that I graduated high school and college and am now pursuing my PhD but most importantly, I touch the lives of thousands of children just like me. I would love to share with them that my success in life started because of them.

I am living this life for a bigger purpose, not for me but for all of you. For the young person who does not think they can make it because life is too complicated and cannot get better, and for the educators and mentors who have the reach and capability to help guide a young person's life onto the right path.

With the mention of those great people, this memoir is also a guide to understanding the backgrounds of children too often misunderstood and, as a result, written off as a societal failure. So, to the people with opportunities to mentor, guide, coach, assist, or help in any way, a young child struggling as the product of their environment, these insights can be critical for you to understand.

Educators must realize that most kids with difficult home lives fit into a few categories. I have a personal list of ten significant categories that I have identified. Knowing these categories will help educators understand and have a higher success rate when connecting with students. Some include but are not limited to physical, mental, and sexual abuse, just to speak of the major ones. But many will overlook the impact of hunger, overachiever pressure, or even sports pressure abuse.

Often, the unknown and less obvious are most detrimental to a child. Even without active and current abuse or neglectful environments, a child can have these situations in their past and still struggle with the lasting effects. As an educator, you must look into the light of compassion and open your mind to see outside the box, only thinking, "this is just a bad kid." There is always more to it if you take the time to look deeper into a child and their current or previous environments.

I look at the decisions that students make through the eyes of my past self. I look at the way they talk and the choices they make. I often ask what it is that drives them to make the decisions they make. As a former special education student and student of an alternative school behavior program, I can step into their shoes and see what is beneath the facade. The keys to reaching a child's inner layer are compassion, respect, understanding, and discipline.

Home Life Categories:

1. Physical Abuse
2. Mental Abuse
3. Sexual Abuse
4. Low Income
5. Negative Environment
6. Hunger
7. Overachiever Pressure

8. Lack of Knowledge

9. Sibling Care

10. Sports Pressure

83% of students say a teacher has boosted their self-esteem and confidence. I was one of many lucky enough to come across teachers and coaches who were caring and compassionate. So often, kids are right at the line of no return, where they must choose one direction or another that could change the course of their life.

One positive seed can alter a child's life or way of thinking. So often, these kids do not understand that a 15-second decision can have a lifetime effect. Others are at a place where one conversation or statement of positive affirmation could help them see their turning point. As I mentioned before, it was a message from a teacher that I thought I hated who delivered that message to me. These words stuck with me and helped me change my life for the better.

Rather you know it or not, you are that teacher. You are the mentor or whoever has that young person's ear at the time. I believe most educators are kind-hearted and genuinely want to help—however, many struggle with understanding the complexity of identifying how they can help. Roughly eight-in-ten U.S. public school teachers (79%) identified as white. Young inner-city, low-income students are likelier to have a white female teacher than any other. Although with good intentions, many struggle with knowing what authentic help looks like.

In schools where more than 75% of students qualify for free or reduced lunch, 17% of teachers are Hispanic, 14% are Black, and 63% are White.

Four out of five teachers, 80%, stated that they often wanted to help but felt that they did not know where to start. Many teachers feel like they lack the proper training to understand and relate to many of their lower-income and inner-city students. Teachers stated that they had approached students with a genuine intention to help them but had said the wrong thing. Building a trust-filled relationship is paramount to the success of connecting with a struggling student. In the past, I have trained teachers using the acronym S.I.R.

S.I.R stands for Spot, Identify, and Relate. When relating to students, we must be patient in their presence. We have to allow them to be who they are, allowing us to see what they truly need. This step is referred to as spotting.

SPOT

Spotting a student that is in need is critical. Students' needs are essential in any student-teacher relationship. Spotting can be done in many ways, and you must understand that you may spot more than one issue within a student. The spotting period has to be combined with relationship building simultaneously. I believe a student will not allow a teacher to spot the actual root cause problem if they have no relationship with the student. What does the student need you to be? As educators, you must be willing to be different and sometimes be what you are not.

As I have researched and learned more about the many signs of abuse, I can see that I was a walking billboard for what a child in need looked like. If my teachers had the training, they might have noticed that I was sexually and physically abused. When spotting a child that may be experiencing abuse, some signs to look out for are inadequate personal hygiene, running away from home, depression, and fear of closeness. As a teacher, if you give students hugs or pats on the back or shoulder for doing something well, pay attention to how they receive that physical contact. If that student recoils or pulls away from any contact, that can be a tell-tale sign.

During my sexual abuse, I did not want to be touched by a stranger, teacher, or family member. I felt closed off from the world at that point. I was also very distracted or distant and did not want to participate in anything fun. Often with children experiencing abuse or neglect, the child will blame themselves. I used to ask myself what I had done to deserve that type of treatment all the time.

There are also instances of children lashing out in anger, avoiding speaking up or reading aloud, falling asleep in class often, and being extra hungry or hiding school-provided food. These are some strong signs of learning disabilities as well as neglect. I know students do not make it easy to help, but as educators or adults, we must try.

Yes, I know we all would like to think that we are always right and know what is best. However, this isn't the case, and we must own that. Sometimes we must allow ourselves to be undisciplined and less strict at the right time. The student must believe that you have their best interest at hand. Yes, you must be stern with students to build respect, but it has to come across as love and care. During your relationship-building, I believe you must allow the student to speak freely in the right moments. You have to hear how they speak, think, and truly feel about certain situations to understand who they are deep down. During the relationship-building phase, you are trying to understand their motivation and what hurts or angers them.

Many of our students may not be comfortable expressing themselves to an adult or an authority figure. I often listen to my students speaking with their peers and steal some of their conversation topics. I do this in an attempt to talk to them about the same topics, which usually creates comfort and relatability for the student. Sometimes it works, and other times it does not. But what I get out of this is catching if they change the way they express themselves with me vs how I heard them express themselves with their friends. Which is the real them? That is who I am seeking; when I feel I have the unfiltered student, then and only then can I truly motivate and teach.

As educators, we teach the whole student and try to guide their entire life. Not just about science, math, reading, and history. But we are teaching identity, self-expression, ethics, morals, and culture. We cannot teach how to think but can encourage how to think freely and independently to the noise of others or situations. We are teaching temperament, self-control, and most importantly, self-worth.

IDENTIFY

The second step is identifying. In this step, you identify by name or act what you detected during the spotting phase. You are identifying the specific need and how you can help. The one thing that we all know is that every student is different. So even if some of their needs are the same, each individual requires different approaches.

Many students like me struggled with allowing people from the outside in to help. One reason was the concern of the person trying to help being judgmental of the situation. I was a student that thought a teacher or mentor would look down on me if they knew the truth. Also, believe it or not, many students are overly protective of their parents or, in many cases, the one parent that is supposed to care for them. They do not want them to be judged, so they will do everything they can to avoid making them look bad. This is where some go wrong. They mean well by helping, but it cannot come in the form of condemning or bashing the parents.

RELATE

The last step is to relate and deliver. You may think this is the easiest step, but I have found this to be one of the most trying. As an educator, it is almost impossible to deliver a message to a student without being able to relate to them. You do not have to come from the same background as your student to relate to them. I had many teachers who had no idea where I had come from. Their lives were not relatable to what I had to live through, but they found a way to understand me. And when they did that, they could speak to me from their heart, without a judging look in their eyes. Relating must be combined with compassion. Compassion often opens your heart to relating, and a kid can see that.

You are the teacher that will change lives. You are in a position of unbelievable power and influence. You have to leave your ego at the door when you enter the classroom and know that this profession you have chosen can be unfair and brutal. It is tiring, stressful, and sometimes unrecognized. In those trying times, remember you are an advocate for greatness, success, and fortitude. You do a job that no one else can do because you chose this job for a reason. Simply stated, you are a superhero.

My mom and I

My mom and Aunt Pam

Lil Freddie and Isaiah

This is either myself or my brother Joe
playing in the hallway.

My mom, her husband Doug.

Lil Freddie and Isaiah

Lil Freddie and Isaiah

Uncle Edward, Lil Freddie,
Isaiah, Uncle Jeff

My grandfather Lil Charlie

My grandfather Lil Charlie shining shoes

Brothers: Keon, Joe and
Taiwan

Big sister Tasha

My brother Wayne

Me and my brother Joe

Older me

Top: brother Wayne, Me, niece Hope, brother Keon, brother Joe Bottom: niece Seray,
mother Amanda, brother Taiwan, sister Tasha, nephew Tevin

Acknowledgements

As with everything I do in life, this first book of three memoirs would not have been possible without the love and support of so many people in my life. So many others made just as much of a sacrifice as I did.

To my son Charles Davis, thank you for taking a beautiful picture for the cover and lending your voice to the audiobook. I love you son, and I know your future will be amazing because you are smart, hardworking, and brilliant. To my son Carter Davis, thank you for helping me design the cover title. I love you son, and if you continue to live your life with as much compassion, love, and motivation as you do right now, the skies are the limit for you kid. Both of you have changed my life for the better, and I am the man I am right now because of you two. I will forever be the best father to you guys that I can be. I will never fail you two. Love, Dad.

My fiancée, Shenika, my love, thank you for holding down the home front while I work for hours every day on this project. Thank you for understanding my need for commitment to this book and for your unwavering love and support. It is your guidance that helped me through so many long nights. I am excited about the journey that awaits us. You are the most beautiful woman, inside and out, that I have ever met. You are truly a blessing in my life.

Thank you to my mother, Amanda Davis, for allowing me to share her stories. I love you mom and thank you for taking the time to give me all the information you did. My grandmother Freddie Davis-Johnson, thank you for being such an amazing inspiration to me my whole life. I hope I am making you proud. I love you and miss you dearly.

To my brothers and sister for allowing me to share their stories, I love you guys, and I am so proud of the growth that you guys have been showing over the past few years. Love. A special thanks to my uncle Keith for all the stories of my father's childhood. Thank you to my Uncle Edward for his stories of my mother's childhood and thank you to my Aunt Pam for the many pictures she shared. Thank you to my friend Tangle for reading so many chapters and giving her honest opinion. I am so grateful for all that had a hand in this process and those I may be leaving out. I am truly blessed to have such a great support system.

I honestly could not have gotten through this process without the brilliance of my Lead Substantive and Copy Editor, Lari-Nicole Kelley. I find it hard to express through words how grateful I truly am to have Nikki on my team. Nikki kept me balanced and motivated from the beginning, and she ensured I could express my entire vision of this project. I appreciate her energy and commitment to delivering a fantastic piece of literature.

Nikki was a Substantive and Copy Editor along with the researcher, finding the answers to all our questions. And I cannot forget to mention her husband, my good friend Andrew. If it were not for Andrew selecting such an amazing woman to be his wife, then our paths would have never crossed.

Then there is my Developmental Editor, Michelle Cerone, whose passion and understanding of my story made me want to partner with her now and in the future. Her professionalism and communication helped to push the book to its highest potential. Not only did she help tremendously, but she also took the time to teach and pass on so much knowledge. Thank you for being great at what you do. I look forward to our future projects.

I want to thank all the many students I have had the chance to speak to. I want to thank all the Professors, Principals, and teachers who have allowed me to share my message with their students. It is you that will change the world. You are the real superheroes.

References

1. Carnegie Foundation Forum On Education And The Economy, Task Force On Teaching As A Profession. A Nation Prepared: Teachers for the 21st Century. Washington, DC: Carnegie Foundation; 1986.

2. Fultz Michael. The displacement of black educators post-Brown: an overview and analysis. History of Education Quarterly. 2004;44(1):1–27.

3. Hudson M, Holmes B. Missing teachers, impaired communities: the unanticipated consequences of Brown v. Board of Education on the African American teaching force at the precollegiate level. Journal of Negro Education. 1994;63(3):388–93.

4. Miller Paul Chamness, Endo Hidehiro. Journey to becoming a teacher: the experiences of students of color. Multicultural Education. 2005;13(1):

5. Stewart Joseph, Meier Kenneth J, England Robert E. In quest of role models: change in black teacher representation in urban school districts, 1968–1986. The Journal of Negro Education. 1989;58(2):140–52.

6. Tillman Linda C. (Un)intended consequences? The impact of the Brown v. Board of Education decision on the employment status of black educators. Education and Urban Society. 2004;36(3):280–303.

Made in the USA
Columbia, SC
07 June 2023

17683915R00128